ICFA Continuing Education

Improving the Investment Decision Process—Better Use of Economic Inputs in Securities Analysis and Portfolio Management

March 31, 1991
Washington, D.C.

Peter L. Bernstein, *Moderator*
David B. Bostian, Jr., CFA
Charles I. Clough, Jr., CFA
Chris P. Dialynas

Jeffrey J. Diermeier, CFA
Elaine Garzarelli
Robert W. Kopprasch, CFA
Stephen K. McNees

Edited by H. Kent Baker, CFA

To obtain an AIMR Publications Catalog or to order additional copies of this publication, turn to page 75 or contact:

AIMR Publications Sales Department
P.O. Box 7947
Charlottesville, VA 22906
Telephone: 804/980-3647
Fax: 804/977-0350

The Association for Investment Management and Research comprises the Institute of Chartered Financial Analysts and the Financial Analysts Federation.

ISBN 1-879087-20-0

Printed in the United States of America

12/29/92

Table of Contents

Foreword

Economic forecasts are key inputs to security valuation and portfolio construction models. Analysts use economic data to develop forecasts of cash flows and discount rates; portfolio managers use economic data to develop expectations of the capital markets, leading to asset allocations. The effective application of economic inputs in the investment process is becoming more important as companies, industries, markets, and economies become more complex and more international in character.

Tremendous volumes of economic data are being generated by increasingly sophisticated computer programs and electronic data collection methods, and investment professionals are consuming the data at an increasing rate. More data are not necessarily better data, however. The information is not always accurate nor relevant, and models developed to use the data often have serious shortcomings. This creates problems for those relying on the data and the forecasting models.

Because it is important for investment professionals to understand the limitations of economic data and forecasting models, AIMR sponsored a seminar entitled *Improving the Investment Decision Process—Better Use of Economic Inputs in Securities Analysis and Portfolio Management*. This is the second proceedings on this topic in the ICFA Continuing Education series, the first being 1985's *Applying Economic Analysis to*

Portfolio Management: Improving the Investment Decision Process. The current proceedings addresses the nature of economic data and describes various approaches to using these data in security valuation and portfolio construction. The proceedings also covers ways to expand the use of economic data to a global portfolio level. We trust you will find this publication valuable.

Many individuals contributed to the success of the seminar and this proceedings. AIMR thanks all of them, with special gratitude to H. Kent Baker, CFA, who edited this proceedings, and Peter L. Bernstein, conference moderator. Their combined wisdom permeates this publication.

The speakers contributing to the seminar were: Peter L. Bernstein, president, Peter L. Bernstein, Inc.; David B. Bostian, Jr., CFA, chief economist and investment strategist, Herzog, Heine, Geduld, Inc.; Charles I. Clough, Jr., CFA, chief investment strategist, Merrill Lynch & Co.; Chris P. Dialynas, managing director, Pacific Investment Management Co.; Jeffrey J. Diermeier, CFA, managing partner, Brinson Partners, Inc.; Elaine Garzarelli, director of quantitative strategies, Lehman Brothers; Robert W. Kopprasch, CFA, senior vice president, Alliance Capital Management L.P.; and Stephen K. McNees, vice president and economist, Federal Reserve Bank of Boston.

Katrina F. Sherrerd, CFA
Vice President
Publications and Research
AIMR

Biographies of Speakers

Peter L. Bernstein is president of Peter L. Bernstein, Inc., economic consultants to institutional investors and corporations. He writes and publishes a twice-monthly analysis of the capital markets and the real economy, *Economics and Portfolio Strategy*, and is founder and consulting editor of *The Journal of Portfolio Management*. Mr. Bernstein previously served as a director, senior vice president, and chairman of the Investment Policy Committee of Shearson/Lehman-American Express and as president and chairman of Bernstein-Macaulay. He is the author of five books, including *Capital Ideas: The Improbable Origins of Modern Wall Street*. He has served as a member of the Overseers' Visiting Committee to the Department of Economics at Harvard and as a trustee and member of the Finance Committee of the College Retirement Equities Fund. Mr. Bernstein is a graduate of Harvard University.

David B. Bostian, Jr., CFA, is chief economist and investment strategist at Herzog, Heine, Geduld, Inc. Previously, he was head of his own consulting firm and was director of market research at two Wall Street firms. Mr. Bostian has participated in such groups as the President's Economic Policy Advisory Board and the White House Conference on Productivity, and he has acted as an advisor to the Bush Administration and the Federal Reserve. Mr. Bostian has been published widely in such publications as the *Financial Analysts Journal* and *The Journal of Portfolio Management*. He is co-author of *Methods and Techniques of Business Forecasting* and author of *World Change*. Mr. Bostian received his bachelor's degree from Davidson College and his M.B.A. from the University of North Carolina at Chapel Hill, where he was a Business Foundation Scholar.

Charles I. Clough, Jr., CFA, is chief investment strategist at Merrill Lynch & Co. Previously, he was director of investment policy and chief strategist at Cowen & Co., director of research and portfolio manager at the Boston Co., portfolio manager at Colonial Management Associates, and vice president and senior research analyst for Donaldson, Lufkin & Jenrette and Alliance Capital Management Co. Mr. Clough has won a place on *Institutional Investor* magazine's All-American Research Team for the past six years. He studied economics at Boston College and received his M.B.A. from the University of Chicago.

Chris P. Dialynas is managing director of Pacific Investment Management Co. As a bond portfolio manager, he shares primary responsibility for the management of assets exceeding $30 billion. Mr. Dialynas is a member of the Board of Directors of the Investment Strategy Group and the Compensation Committee at Pacific Investment Management. He has published articles on a variety of topics related to fixed-income investing. He received his B.A. from Pomona College, where he studied economics, and his M.B.A. in finance from the University of Chicago.

Jeffrey J. Diermeier, CFA, is managing partner at Brinson Partners, Inc., a global institutional money management firm headquartered in Chicago. He is responsible for all aspects of the management of actively managed U.S. equity assets. He manages a staff of 12 investment researchers as well as the trading staff, and he participates in the development and implementation of the firm's global asset allocation investment strategy and business plans. Previously, Mr. Diermeier was managing director of asset allocation and investment manager of the Multi-Asset Portfolio Fund. He is a member of the Board of Directors of the Investment Analysts of Chicago, and he has served as ad hoc referee for the *Financial Analysts Journal* and as a member of the University of Wisconsin Business Alumni Board. Mr. Diermeier attended the University of Wisconsin, where he received B.B.A. and M.B.A. degrees.

Elaine Garzarelli is director of quantitative strategies at Lehman Brothers. She has been named to *Institutional Investor* magazine's All-American Research Team in the quantitative analysis category for the past eight years. She initially developed her sector analysis methodology for predicting industry earnings and the stock market while working as a corporate profit economist. Ms. Garzarelli currently uses a mathematical approach to stock market timing and industry selection in managing a mutual fund, the Sector Portfolio. She was featured as "Business Woman of the Year" in *Fortune* magazine in 1987 and in *Business Week*'s "What's In" list for 1992. Ms. Garzarelli is a Ph.D. candidate at New York University.

Robert W. Kopprasch, CFA, is senior vice president of Alliance Capital Management L.P., where he oversees quantitative and security specific research. Prior to joining Alliance in 1992, Mr. Kopprasch was a managing director and portfolio manager for Hyperion Capital, responsible for the firm's investment research. Previously, he was co-director of financial strategies at Goldman Sachs and a director and manager of the Bond Portfolio Analysis Hedge Group at Salomon Brothers, Inc. He has published numerous articles and periodicals on fixed-income market research. Mr. Kopprasch holds a Ph.D. in finance from Rensselaer Polytechnic Institute.

Stephen K. McNees is vice president and economist at the Federal Reserve Bank of Boston. His responsibilities include briefing the president and board of directors on the economy and economic policy. His major research interest has been in the evaluation of economic forecasts and assessing the role of macroeconometric policy for the President's Council of Economic Advisers. Mr. McNees has also served as a consultant to the Congressional Budget Office and the General Accounting Office. He is currently an associate editor of the *International Journal of Forecasting* and a referee for several professional journals and the National Science Foundation. He has taught at Harvard University, Northeastern University, Massachusetts Institute of Technology, and Williams College. He completed his bachelor's degree at Swarthmore College and received his Ph.D. from Massachusetts Institute of Technology.

Improving the Investment Decision Process—Better Use of Economic Inputs in Securities Analysis and Portfolio Management: An Overview

H. Kent Baker, CFA
Professor and Chair
Department of Finance and Real Estate
Kogod College of Business Administration
The American University

Economic inputs are useful in the analysis of individual securities, portfolio construction, and asset allocation. In recent years, the effective use of economic inputs has become more complex. Viewing economic analysis and forecasting from only a domestic perspective is no longer appropriate. Because globalization affects most U.S. companies and industries, analysts and portfolio managers cannot ignore its impact when developing economic forecasts or capital market assumptions.

The presentations in this proceedings provide an important update to the first examination of this topic, a seminar entitled *Improving the Investment Decision Process: Applying Economic Analysis to Portfolio Management*, presented by the Institute of Chartered Financial Analysts in 1984. The underlying theme of the current publication is that economic inputs are critical ingredients in the investment decision process. Yet investment professionals often have difficulty making accurate economic forecasts.

As the following statement from the *Economic Report of the President* (February 1992) suggests, however, forecasting is both a science and an art: "Economic forecasting is an imprecise science. . . . Unexpected events and policy changes can cause actual events to be substantially different from the forecast. Forecasts are based largely on predictions about human behavior, usually taking previous patterns of behavior as a guide. But human behavior is complex, difficult to predict, and subject to change. People do not always respond the same way, or with the same speed, in what appear to be similar circumstances. Hence, uncertainty remains about the outlook of the economy."

The presentations in this proceedings begin by reviewing economic forecasts, their risks, alternative forecasting methods, and the accuracy of macroeconomic forecasts. Then, the presentations focus on constructing portfolios holding only domestic securities and on applying forecasts to fixed-income and equity analysis. The discussion next expands to a global context and addresses using international economic inputs in portfolio construction and asset allocation. The final presentation shows how an investment strategist moves from raw data to refined forecast to global portfolio allocation.

The Nature of Effective Forecasts

According to Bostian, the use of economic inputs in securities analysis and portfolio management is one of the areas of greatest deficiency in the financial community today. He provides an overview of the forecasting process, discusses the risks in economic forecasting, and addresses the importance of disciplines for accurate economic forecasting. Bostian also examines what is and is not possible in forecasting, alternative forecasting methods, and international influences on domestic forecasting. He considers forecasting the economic cycle the principal challenge because it influences other variables such as inflation, interest rates, and profits.

One of Bostian's key tenets is that economic forecasting is both a science and an art. He stresses that forecasting reflects the blending of statistical facts with judgment about human behavior. Many economic forecasters fail because of three human weaknesses: linear perception, group think, and messenger syndrome. Forecasts also go astray because of inaccurate data and erroneous economic theories. Over time, the science element may come to dominate the human judgment element of forecasting.

Another key tenet is that consistently accurate forecasting of the economic cycle requires a decision-oriented discipline to help avoid psychological pitfalls, erroneous data, and faulty theories. Bostian calls his discipline the Macro-Economic Index (MEI). He shows that the MEI, which has 26 independent economic variables, has had a strong record of signaling both recessions and recoveries during the past four decades. A rate of change basis is one of the best methods for expressing such a discipline. He believes that consensus, scenario, and historical approaches have value but only as supplements to decision-oriented disciplines.

Bostian concludes by noting the international influences on domestic forecasting. His international tenet is first to make forecasts based on variables that have been valid from a domestic standpoint and then change the forecasts based on international considerations.

The Accuracy of Macroeconomic Forecasts

McNees examines five questions:
- Who are the best forecasters?
- How large are forecast errors?
- How have errors varied over time?
- Is forecast accuracy improving?
- What is the best forecasting technique?

He notes that no single forecaster dominates for all or even most variables that interest investment professionals. The ranking of top forecasters depends on several variables, including the horizon of the forecasts and whether the forecast involves levels or changes. In fact, forecasts are similar among the most prominent forecasters. McNees says the size of forecast errors depends largely on the variable being forecasted and the forecast period. Forecast accuracy also depends on the release date. Revised forecasts are generally more accurate than preliminary forecasts because they are based on more recent data.

McNees notes a gradual improvement in forecasting accuracy over time because of constant competition, improvements in forecasting techniques, changes in the structure of the economy, and increases in the quantity of data available. This gradual improvement is not guaranteed to continue, however.

He maintains that naive models are hard to beat as the best forecasting technique for variables such as interest rates and stock market prices. For macroeconomic variables, including unemployment and the consumer price index, prominent forecasters beat statistical rules of thumb, but the margin of superiority is small.

From Forecast to Portfolio Construction

Bernstein reviews some concepts about diversification developed by Harry Markowitz. Bernstein stresses that the objective in going from forecast to portfolio is to compose a set of assets with low covariance; that is, the task is to reduce risk while sustaining expected return. This process begins with the capital market line, which Bernstein uses to show how risk–return relationships can change over time. For example, from 1926 to 1991, a portfolio of 60 percent S&P 500 stocks and 40 percent long-term bonds offered a return premium relative to the risk imposed. From 1979 to 1991, however, this portfolio provided returns too small relative to the risks. The deterioration in the performance of the 60/40 portfolio partly resulted from an upward shift in covariance; the benefits of diversification diminished after 1979 because of a higher correlation between stock and bond returns. Bernstein then presents a model for determining the correlation between the two asset classes.

Another route from forecast to portfolio construction is through the expected equity risk premium, or the excess of equity returns over bond returns. Bernstein suggests buying stocks and selling bonds if the spread is wider than normal. If equities are expected to outperform bonds by a smaller amount than usual, then the opposite strategy (sell stocks and buy bonds) is appropriate.

Bernstein concludes by noting that the major lesson of financial history is the instability of most relationships. This lesson suggests that managers should test all models and assumptions often to see if they still hold.

Constructing Fixed-Income Portfolios

Dialynas develops a relative risk framework for using economic inputs to construct fixed-income portfolios. Because no simple, reliable rules exist for using economic inputs, portfolio managers must be aware of their confidence levels in the inputs and their own biases in forecasting. He also provides a guide to bond portfolio management.

Within this framework, portfolio managers must first understand the link from an economic forecast to an interest rate forecast. Second, they must integrate a long-term, or secular trend, forecast with a shorter term, cyclical forecast. Third, they must understand how the forecast affects the attractiveness of bond classes and individual bonds.

Dialynas notes that the goal of bond portfolio managers is to add value. Although value can be added in many ways, the most potent method is usually a duration strategy—the implementation of an interest rate forecast. Other methods of adding value include sector selection and the choice of the distribution of cash flows along the yield curve.

In his discussion of risk measurement of bond portfolios, Dialynas observes that conventional measures of risk, such as average maturity and average quality, are inadequate. He also shows the potential deficiency of duration as a risk measurement and examines the importance of volatility expectations in bond portfolio management.

Dialynas concludes with a simplified guide to bond selection. This guide shows how portfolio managers can use economic inputs in the bond management process to select sectors and securities and to express their confidence in the inputs through the relative volatility of the portfolios.

Selecting Fixed-Income Securities

The investment approach to fixed-income security selection presented by Kopprasch differs from that suggested by Dialynas. Although both try to add value, Kopprasch does not focus on forecasts of interest rate movements and then adjust duration. Instead, his firm tries to outperform benchmarks through sector and security selection rather than through interest rate anticipation.

Kopprasch describes the approach his firm uses to move from forecasts to selection of individual fixed-income securities. This approach applies fundamental and quantitative analysis to determine which sectors offer the greatest risk-adjusted returns. His firm tries to get an optimum duration structure relative to its forecasts and to the level of confidence in them.

Kopprasch then turns his attention to mortgage-backed securities. The selection process begins by estimating prepayment rates for various types of mortgage-backed securities. He examines the importance of prepayment forecasts and identifies three economic factors that generate prepayments:

▨ The *transfer effect* occurs as workers move to areas experiencing economic growth.

▨ The *income effect* leads homeowners to increase their housing expenditures and "trade up."

▨ The *rate effect* encourages homeowners to prepay their mortgages if their rates are high but current mortgage rates are low (or to restrain prepayments if their rates are low but mortgage rates are high).

The next step in the investment process is to use quantitative analysis (option-adjusted spreads, expected total returns, and effective duration and convexity) to determine the attractiveness of individual securities and their potential role in a portfolio. The process of selecting individual securities in the mortgage market is difficult because each security is unique. The key economic time series for mortgage-backed securities valuation are interest rates, housing data, and nonhousing statistics such as personal income and consumer confidence. Finally, the formal portfolio formation process begins by combining risk and return estimates into the optimal portfolio.

Selecting Equity Securities

Garzarelli identifies four major factors that move the equity markets: sentiment, the economy, Federal Reserve policy, and valuation. Each factor has about the same degree of effect on overall market movements—25 percent. Garzarelli explains how she developed her econometric models and hints at some variables contained in them. For example, key variables in the economy are earnings, industrial production, and real gross domestic product, measured on a rate-of-change basis.

Based on these models, Garzarelli makes several observations about the U.S. economy, equity markets, and various types of investments. She argues that signs of recovery make the economy's prospects look good but with a higher level of unemployment, especially in the banking and insurance industries and among attorneys. She expects the stock market will keep going up (possibly a Dow of 4000) until the economy's growth rate starts to peak; then it will begin to slow. She expects the market to peak during the third quarter of 1993. Garzarelli also states that the best industries to hold in mid-1992 are the cyclical groups. When the S&P 500 earnings slow again, possibly in mid-1993, foods, drugs, and more defensive industries should become attractive. Currently, investments such as real estate, gold, oriental rugs, and jewelry are not attractive.

Using International Economic Inputs

Diermeier deals with expanding the use of economics to a global portfolio level. He briefly discusses strategic asset allocation techniques and a standardized valuation model before examining global portfolio construction.

Diermeier notes four strategic asset allocation techniques: comparative valuation, business cycle anticipation, liquidity/flow of funds, and technical analysis. He focuses on comparative valuation. Using this approach requires estimating some level of intrinsic value across securities or asset classes, comparing them, considering risk, and building portfolios. To estimate the value of an asset, he uses a standardized three-stage valuation model consisting of discounted value in growth to normal stage, discounted value in the normal growth stage, and discounted value in the mature stage. This estimate of intrinsic value is then compared to the market price. He also discusses how to measure economic growth and capital market returns.

Diermeier identifies three challenges unique to building a global portfolio—currency allocation, risky asset allocation, and decision hierarchy (country versus security)—and discusses how to deal with each.

Developing a Recommendation for a Global Portfolio

Clough, a global market strategist, develops forecasts and provides asset allocation recommendations for global portfolios. He offers three guidelines for designing any investment portfolio: Know what you do not know, try to assess where change occurs, and develop a discipline to determine where the consensus might be wrong.

Clough makes many observations about global economic and market conditions, including:

- A worldwide credit contraction is under way, which will affect economic growth, bank rates, bond yields, and price–earnings ratios around the world.
- Emerging cycles in the industrialized world are visible in North America, but not in Japan, Europe, or in countries where the economy is still weakening.
- Capital will flow to Eastern Europe, Latin America, India, and China by the mid-1990s.
- The 1990s will bring lower financial market and cash returns than in the 1980s.
- The worldwide cost of capital is falling because all industrialized nations are in the backside of their real estate credit cycles.

The Nature of Effective Forecasts

David B. Bostian, Jr., CFA
Chief Economist and Investment Strategist
Herzog, Heine, Geduld, Inc.

Any technique for making economic forecasts should have a discipline to help avoid psychological pitfalls and those related to erroneous data and theories. A discipline serves as a frame of reference to force the forecaster to identify decision points. This discipline is required to take available data and bring them into coherent focus.

Forecasting is both a science and an art. On the surface, that statement does not sound very profound. But the longer you are in this business, the more you will see the truth in it. No sure technique and no one econometric model can forecast the economy or select individual stocks, construct portfolios, or even allocate assets. At some point, a model that has worked well in the past will suddenly cease working. This is primarily because in forecasting, we are dealing with human behavior.

You should read the *Economic Report of the President*, published annually by the Government Printing Office, not only for its substance but also for its interweaving of politics and economics. Economics is political. It is not a quantitative or statistical discipline that can be analyzed in a vacuum, free from what happens on the political front.

Over the years, these economic reports have varied substantially in their degree of cockiness or humility. The following is from the 1992 *Economic Report*: "Economic forecasting is an imprecise science. . . . Unexpected events and policy changes can cause actual events to be substantially different from the forecast. Forecasts are based largely on predictions about human behavior, usually taking previous patterns of behavior as a guide. But human behavior is complex, difficult to predict, and subject to change. People do not always respond the same way, or with the same speed, in what appear to be similar circumstances. Hence, uncertainty remains about the outlook for the economy." Having this statement come from the *Economic Report of the President* is important because it emphasizes the art of forecasting. It has a human element.

The art-form aspect of forecasting reflects the blending of statistical facts with judgments about human behavior based on insights derived from both experience and intuition. One might conjecture, as we develop fifth-generation computers and artificial intelligence systems, that the science element will become more dominant. An intriguing article in a recent issue of the *Financial Analysts Journal* pointed out the exciting potential of using "fuzzy neural systems" for forecasting.[1] These systems use fifth-generation computers and artificial intelligence, in which the machine starts to think, possibly even in the irrational ways humans think. Conceivably, we will develop fuzzy neural systems for forecasting the economy, and maybe then it will become more science than art. This remains to be seen.

Forecasting the economic cycle is the dominant challenge. Forecasting interest rates and inflation is important, but they derive from the movement of the economic cycle itself. The data that go into the forecast are a tremendous challenge in timeliness. To have any element of science, you must grapple with data, and a major challenge is to determine the data's quality. Assume you have developed some data that appear to forecast the economy, interest rates, or inflation. The validity of the data deteriorates over time. For example, about a decade ago, many people focused on weekly money supply figures. Using these figures, they tried to figure out whether to buy or sell stocks and bonds or the implications for the economy. We have moved away from money supply figures and now look at payroll employment or other data. Eventually forecasts will be proven wrong because we are dealing with a human element and/or erroneous data.

[1]F.S. Wong, P.Z. Wang, T.H. Goh, and B.K. Quek, "Fuzzy Neural Systems for Stock Selection," *Financial Analysts Journal* (January/February 1992):47–52, 74.

Understanding Risks in Economic Forecasting

Many economic forecasters fail because of three human weaknesses. First is *linear perception*—the human tendency to remember the past and extrapolate it into the future in a straight line. The stock market went up from 1982 to 1987, with similar trends for the bond market, corporate profits, and so forth. Events since autumn 1987 make obvious that most things do not move in straight lines.

Second is *group think*. This deals with the human tendency to want to feel comfortable. Whether economists, strategists, or analysts, people tend to gravitate toward a consensus view because it is comfortable. The problem is the risk that comes from subconsciously gravitating into a consensus view because you do not want to appear to be an outsider.

The third human weakness is the *messenger syndrome*. If the message is good, this is not necessarily a problem, but in Greek and Roman times, the messenger who brought bad news to the emperor was "shot" (i.e., speared). Many economists had given up forecasting a recession by late 1989 and early 1990 to avoid the discomfort of delivering unpleasant messages that had repeatedly proven incorrect.

Another type of risk in economic forecasting is the data. Erroneous data can lead to trouble no matter how sophisticated the model or skilled the intuition about the data. For example, the financial press carried much commentary about how, as the current recession approached, the Labor Department was creating phantom jobs by extrapolating the past into the future based on newly started businesses. Based on this information, the Commerce Department decided these jobs created personal income, and if personal income was growing, the economy was healthy. Unfortunately, the whole concept was a statistical mirage. Michael Boskin, chairman of President Bush's Council of Economic Advisers, has spearheaded an effort to upgrade the accuracy of government statistics. That may do as much for our ability to have better forecasts in the future as anything mentioned thus far.

A third type of risk in economic forecasting is faulty economic theories. Not every economic theory is false, but the truth is so complex in an advanced economy in which many humans have different dispositions that no single economic theory can encompass everything. Thus, we have many economic theories. Keynesian economics, for example, basically deals with government spending. With the deficit at its current size, the government cannot stimulate the economy as it did in the past. Another theory, monetarist economics, focuses on money supply: The growth rate of the monetary aggregates is the primary determinate of economic growth, the rate of inflation, and so forth. Milton Friedman, based on his monetary observations, forecasted in the mid-1980s soaring inflation and a relapse into recession. This forecast preceded a period of economic growth and declining inflation. Still other economists cling to supply-side economics.

Many economists develop their own economic theory, and mine is called productivity economics, which appears alien to other theories. This approach emphasizes knowledge, motivation, investment, and energy as the driving forces of economic growth. It could be called liberal arts economics. To understand and forecast the economy, do not look at it in Keynesian, monetary, or supply-side frameworks; try to figure out how the economy really works. It functions because of knowledge, motivation, and investment—whether in people, plant, or machinery—and in inverse relation to the cost of energy.

Effective Economic Forecasts

To be effective, an economic forecast must be reasonably accurate. Any forecasting technique for the economy should have a discipline to help avoid psychological pitfalls and those related to erroneous data and theories. This does not contradict my commentary about the importance of art or judgment or even intuition in the forecasting process. Instead, a discipline serves as a frame of reference to force the forecaster to identify decision points. Some discipline is needed to take whatever data are available and bring them into coherent focus.

The discipline I use, the Macro-Economic Index (MEI), consists of 26 independent economic variables. Its record is exceptional in signaling both recessions and recoveries. **Figure 1** is the monthly plot of the MEI since 1950. The top panel shows the coincident economic index, which is based on industrial production, employees on nonagricultural payrolls, and so forth. It is a real-time measure of the economy, much more so than gross national product (GNP) or gross domestic product (GDP). The shaded bands represent recessions as officially defined after the fact by the National Bureau of Economic Research (NBER).

The MEI represents an attempt to avoid the pitfalls most economists encounter. It differs from the government's Leading Economic Indicators (LEI) by incorporating a wider array of data—26 components as opposed to 11—including measures of interest rates and profits, and using a rate-of-change rather than cumulative basis to calculate the components.

The lower panel of Figure 1 shows how the cyclical turning points are identified. Based on history,

Figure 1. Composite Index of Four Coincident Indicators
(with Bostian Macro-Economic Index signals)

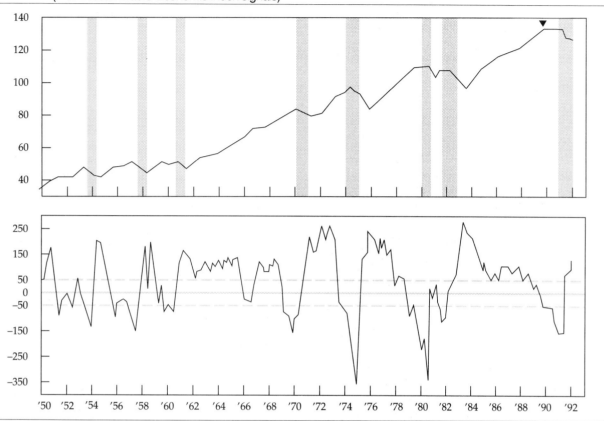

Source: Bostian Economic Research.

Notes: Data based on information from Bureau of Economic Analysis. Last observations January 1992 (top graph) and February 1992 (bottom graph). Shaded areas represent recessions as defined by the National Bureau of Economic Research.

I developed two thresholds: +50, where the index moves into an expansion mode, and –50, where it moves into a recession mode. These signals, of course, are not perfect. Figure 1 shows a down arrow in August 1989, in advance of the date when the recession officially began. NBER has not officially determined when and if the recession ended.

The MEI removes emotion from the forecasting process and, based on the breadth of its measurement of the real and financial economy, it is able to circumvent bad data that distort various individual economic variables from time to time. Nonetheless, judgment is still required in assessing the probable amplitude and duration of cyclical movements and other unique characteristics of each economic cycle. For example, I considered excessive debt to be the unique characteristic of the recent economic downturn.

I am not suggesting you must use the MEI. My message is to have a discipline that uses data on a rate-of-change basis. The MEI's forecasting profile can be approximated by expressing the movement of the leading indicators on a rate-of-change basis. The upper panel of **Figure 2** shows the LEI, which missed

the onset of the most recent recession. In the lower panel, the data are expressed on a year-to-year percent change basis. Although the signals are not always clearly defined, this rate-of-change approach revealed extremely weak economic momentum in the summer of 1990, even though the reported leading indicators data were still making new highs as the recession approached.

Considering that the post-November 1982 economic expansion was setting longevity records in the summer of 1990, and with a progressively weaker response to even greater increments of corporate and consumer indebtedness, forecasting a recession should not have been difficult for most economists. In retrospect, the fact that so many economists missed the recession is amazing. Probably one problem was that they had forecast two or three recessions that did not occur during the record-setting expansion, so they became gun-shy. Apparently, the recession was difficult to forecast because, in combination with other perceptual problems, economists focused on the upward movement of the leading indicators. Although the Middle East conflict did not

Figure 2. Leading Indicators Index

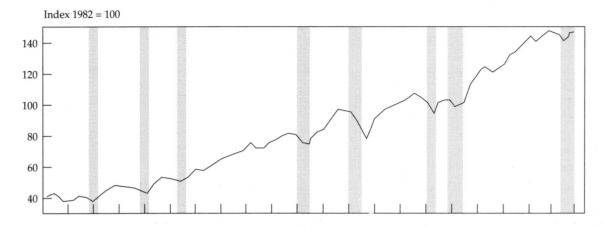

Index 1982 = 100

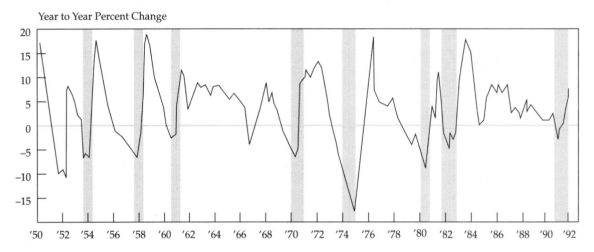

Year to Year Percent Change

Source: Crandall, Pierce & Co.

Notes: Data based on information from Bureau of Economic Analysis. Last observation January 1992. Shaded areas represent recessions as defined by the National Bureau of Economic Research.

cause the recession, it did initially exacerbate it.

Accurate forecasting of the economic cycle requires a decision-oriented discipline. One of the best methods for expressing such a discipline is on a rate-of-change basis. Looking at things on a rate-of-change basis identifies when an absolute series is about to change direction. A business needs time to prepare for a recession or a recovery, and in the investment business, you frequently need time to change your portfolio stance.

Knowing what is and is not possible in forecasting is important. Forecasting the economic cycle is possible. Forecasting the amplitude and duration of an economic expansion or an economic contraction is more difficult. These particular points require several judgmental observations. Certainly the amplitude, or the strength of the recovery, has much to do with whether it reaches extremes. Experience has taught me never to forecast individual statistics, such

as payroll employment, because the numbers are continually revised. Forecasting exogenous events also is not possible. Think about what would happen if a sudden coup occurs in Russia and Yeltsin goes to the Gulag. Geopolitical shocks cannot be forecast.

Alternative Forecasting Methods

Economists use a variety of methods for forecasting the economy and market behavior. *Consensus forecasting* has become popular in recent years. The consensus for 1992 was only 1.6 percent growth in real GDP. Consensus forecasting helps in understanding the "mind of the market." When something different from what the market thinks occurs, the result is big moves in stock and bond markets or in individual securities. But the mind of the market can be right.

The weakness of consensus forecasting is that it can miss critical turning points. The challenge is to try to look at the mind of the market and understand what it is. To use consensus forecasting to explore the mind of the market, ask "What is wrong with this?" If something is wrong with the consensus, that is where the markets move when the adjustment occurs. *Blue Chip Economic Indicators*, a monthly survey of more than 50 economists, has become widely recognized for its consensus economic forecasts. Nevertheless, the *Blue Chip* consensus missed the severe economic downturn in 1982 and the onset of the 1990–91 recession. Otherwise, the record is good.

Scenario analysis is a sophisticated way to manipulate economic variables, often with the aid of a computer, to create different outcomes to which probabilities can be assigned. Strategically, it is useful to consider scenarios that are at odds with a most probable forecast so as to be alert to adverse events and cognizant of the risk that might attend such adverse outcomes. Unfortunately, the multiple scenarios can also lead to a paralysis in decision making because of the many computer printouts reflecting different events that could happen. Which do you act on?

Historical methods assume the past can be used to predict the future. The past is not always prologue, but it provides norms against which to judge what is happening. **Figure 3** presents six indicators. The average for the past six cycles is considered the norm. The leading indicators moved up a little more sharply than the norm, then went laterally, and now they are moving up again, but they are basically tracking history. Real durable goods orders, industrial production, and total employment look different from the norm, but now they are right on the historical track.

Some of these indicators reflect an artificial spurt of euphoria following the apparent success of Operation Desert Storm. This surge in economic activity spiked some of the series up from what would have been a normal recessionary path. When they came back down to where they would have been without Desert Storm, economists said, "Here comes a double-dip recession." It was not a double dip; it was the economic data moving back into a normal recessionary pattern.

The index of consumer sentiment and the housing starts series are tracking below their historical paths, which may reflect some longer term secular problems dealing with debt, demographics, and so forth.

The consensus, scenario, and historical approaches have value, but they seldom provide actionable conclusions about the future. Judgment is

still required. Such approaches allow comparisons of a forecast with what has been the historical norm and identification of possible bias in the deviations, which may be justified.

Evaluating Forecasts

Evaluating forecasts is a continuous process. To be successful in applying economics, focus on what will happen in the future, not what happened in the past. Ask whether something is different out there. In forecasting market data or economic data, ask whether the data contain some knowledge you may not have. This is the continuing battle between what you perceive and know and what the market perceives and knows, and both can be right on occasion.

The easiest way to identify trend change is to use rate-of-change data. Take any series important to an analyst's or portfolio manager's success, and use some method to smooth the data—a 10-day, 10-week, or 10-year moving average, perhaps—and plot the differential between the data and the moving average. Look at the performance of that data during the past 10 or 20 years or however long the history is available. This simple approach is the ultimate pragmatism. If something starts to happen in the data, it will keep you asking why.

Occasionally, the data can be wrong and you can be right. Checking forecasts for consistency and bias is difficult but important. An econometric approach permits a history-based check to be made. If the economy is supposed to expand and interest rates are supposed to go up, but your forecast has interest rates coming down, you may be right. Figure out why something that is historically inconsistent appears to be occurring. Clearly, judgment is the ultimate criterion.

Use of Economic Inputs in Security Analysis

Economic inputs are obviously useful in the analysis of individual securities and the construction of portfolios, as well as in asset allocation. As stated earlier, however, with regard to economic forecasting, use of economic inputs involves as much art (or judgment) as science. Economic relationships can be quantified in almost limitless correlations if mathematical sophistication is more important than accurate forecasts.

Trying to quantify an economic input in forecasting an individual security is a tricky exercise. For example, the revenues of a capital goods company can be correlated with a component of the national income accounts such as capital spending. Nonetheless, capital spending must be accurately projected,

Figure 3. The Business Cycle: Selected Indicators

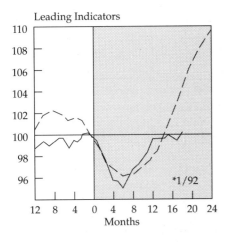

Leading Indicators

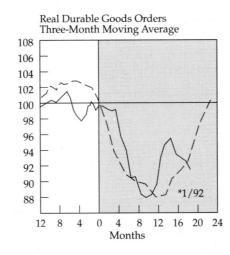

Real Durable Goods Orders
Three-Month Moving Average

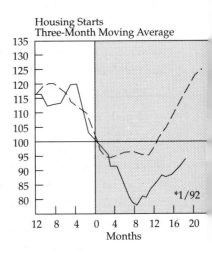

Housing Starts
Three-Month Moving Average

Total Employment
Nonagricultural, Establishment

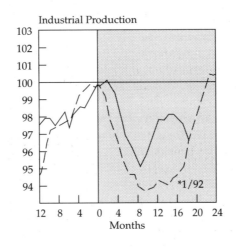

Industrial Production

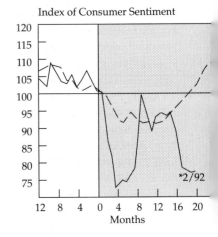

Index of Consumer Sentiment

——— Current Cycle
– – – Average of Previous Six Cycles
0 = Business Cycle Peak

Source: Crandall, Pierce & Co.

Notes: Shaded areas represent the 24 months after the business cycle peak. Current cycle peak = July 1990.

*Indicates last observation of current cycle.

and then, assuming the historical correlation holds with revenues, judgments must be made about possible changes in margins, tax rates, and so forth. Finally, it is necessary to judge what price–earnings multiple the market will apply to the resulting earnings assumption. In my opinion, accurately quantifying the macroeconomic inputs to security analysis will always be difficult. Successful stock selection will always have its "artistic" elements.

John Maynard Keynes addressed the security selection problem by comparing investing to a beauty contest: "Each competitor (investor) has to pick, not those faces which he himself finds the prettiest, but those he thinks likeliest to catch the fancy of the other competitors, all of whom are looking at the problem from the same point of view."[2]

Group and sector selection will become more dominant in professional money management in the 1990s. When portfolios are constructed based on

[2]Peter Bernstein and David Bostian, in *Methods and Techniques of Business Forecasting*, eds. William F. Butler, Robert A. Kavesh, and Robert B. Platt (Englewood Cliffs, N.J.: Prentice Hall, 1974).

group or sector themes, economic inputs may become more statistically significant in the selection process. The factors affecting capital goods stocks, consumer stocks, or oil stocks are much more easily correlated than influences on individual stocks in a larger universe. One company might have problems, but if the group or sector correlation has merit, it might do well.

Figure 4 shows the ratio of prices of capital goods stocks to prices of consumer goods stocks during the past several decades. An unsustainable market disequilibrium has developed between these two major sectors. Capital goods relative performance surpassed that of consumer goods at the end of the 1970s, and then the pendulum swung to an even more extreme position favoring consumer goods stocks in the 1980s. Capital goods stocks may have gone up, but their upward movement is so minute that this ratio has continued to plunge.

Now that the mathematical relationship between the capital goods sector and the consumer goods sector has reached an unsustainable extreme, a weighty array of fundamental factors argues for a major reversal, in favor of overperformance of capital goods equities. These fundamental factors range from market measures to economic factors to demographic trends to government policies. The risk–reward matrix in **Table 1** highlights the reasons portfolio managers should seriously consider increasing the portfolio weighting in the capital goods sector and reducing the weighting in the consumer goods sector. The six factors (market, economics, productivity, profit, demographics, and government policy) imply negative conclusions about the outlook for consumer stocks, possibly mitigated by new markets

abroad, and positive conclusions for the capital goods sector. The implications of this potentially major portfolio shift are incredible risk and reward.

Whether this transition to capital goods stocks will be gradual or more sudden is difficult to ascertain. One possible "sudden" catalyst could be a sustained rise in industrial commodity prices. Capital goods profitability could be surprisingly strong even in the slow economic recovery most economists anticipated. A vigorous economic expansion could produce astounding earnings gains for many capital goods companies.

Most people on Wall Street value the equity market using dividend discount models, historical price–earnings multiples, normalized price–earnings multiples, dividend yields, book values, and so forth, all of which indicate the market has been overvalued. I look at stocks relative to GNP (now GDP), or the ongoing value of the economy. **Figure 5** shows the occasional secular overvaluation and undervaluation of equities. Overvaluation is considered to occur when the market value of all New York Stock Exchange stocks exceeds 70 percent of GNP; undervaluation is below 40 percent. We are now headed back toward overvaluation.

Figure 5. Bostian Equity Valuation/GNP Model
(GDP optional)

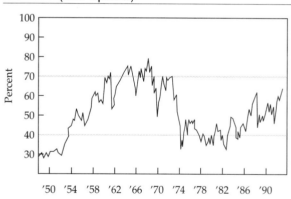

Source: Bostian Economic Research.

Notes: Data based on information from the New York Stock Exchange and the U.S. Commerce Department. Last observation February 1992 est.

International events also influence domestic forecasting, but mixing domestic and international forecast variables can be confusing. I first make forecasts based on variables that have been valid from a domestic standpoint. Then, as a separate exercise, I modify the forecast based on pertinent international considerations. The international realm introduces many unpredictabilities because some economies and political structures have no precedent domesti-

Figure 4. Ratio of Capital Goods/Consumer Goods Stock Prices

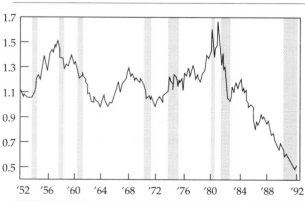

Source: Crandall, Pierce & Co.

Notes: Data based on information from Standard & Poor's Corp. Last observation February 1992. Shaded areas represent recessions as defined by the National Bureau of Economic Research.

Table 1. Factors Affecting Consumer and Capital Stocks

Consumer Stocks Risk Factors	Capital Stocks Reward Factors
Market • High relative P/E[a] • Lower dividend yield • 10-year overperformance • Institutions overweighted now	Market • Low relative P/E[a] • Higher dividend yields • 10-year underperformance • Institutions underweighted now
Economics (consumer spending) • Consumer heavily indebted implies weaker spending in recovery • Consumer purchase mix downscaled by necessity • Home real estate weak	Economics (capital spending) • Corporate competitiveness heavily dependent on capital investment • Emerging world economy implies need for capital exports • Infrastructure rebuilding needed
Productivity • Low-productivity industries • Higher labor costs (services)	Productivity • High-productivity industries • Lower labor costs (manufacturing)
Profit • Profit vulnerability to consumer and government action	Profit • Profit resilience in recession implies strong rebound
Demographics • Aging population implies weaker consumer economy and slower household formation	Demographics • Aging population implies higher savings and capital investment
Government Policy • Anticonsumption tax policy expected	Government Policy • Pro-investment initiatives expected

Source: Bostian Economic Research.

[a]Relative to S&P 500 Index P/E.

cally. International influences, however, should make investing in the 1990s more challenging.

Conclusion

Investment management and research will experience a period of unprecedented innovation and excitement as the 21st century approaches. New disciplines and techniques will be developed and for brief periods will appear to be ultimate solutions to the investment challenges we all face. Keep in mind, however, that the human element in both the economic and investment realms will remain. Implicit in that advice is the need to remember that judgment will always be necessary in achieving "effective forecasts."

Question and Answer Session

David B. Bostian, Jr., CFA

Question: Until the theory of rational expectations, most economic theories did not consider how much information economic agents have. Keynes said that as the money supply increases, the economy becomes more liquid and therefore interest rates go down. Today, when the money supply increases and the economy gets more liquid, interest rates tend to go up. To what extent do you think the markets respond to the information?

Bostian: A substantial driving force of the bull market in equities has been the demand/supply factor. A lot of liquidity that did not want to be receiving 3.5 percent or 4 percent as a return for short-term money is going into the market. If stocks are moving, money tends to go there. While bonds were moving, until the recent sell-off, it went there. That is a human element, not sophisticated economic analysis. It is a matter of seeing cash returns going down, and something that is appreciating, whether it be stocks or bonds, creating higher returns.

The movement of the market over the short to intermediate term is not always rational economically. Ultimately, whatever the fundamental or economic truth may be will determine where values reside for the stock and bond markets. The opportunity for rationality in the market is there, whether it be the market in general or stocks or sectors. The efficient market theory has some big holes, certainly over the short to intermediate term. That presents opportunities for people like us to do our portfolio management, investment strategy,

and security selection.

Question: Although we can measure the quantitative aspects of securities to an ever greater degree, the soft, unmeasurable qualitative factors seem to have a greater impact on prices. Please comment.

Bostian: Both in economics and investment strategy, you need to be aware of qualitative factors—or at least try to figure out what plausible factors exist about which the market is unaware. If the market does become aware of these factors, it may buy the argument. Most people follow conventional approaches to forecasting, which is not where to get insights that produce greater-than-average returns. The judgmental aspects are extremely important.

Question: You are on record as being very hopeful about the outlook, but what about the debt overhang? To what extent do you think it will inhibit economic growth during the next 5 to 10 years? What sort of inhibition will this problem be on the economy?

Bostian: This question allows me to give both a quantitative and a qualitative answer. Quantitatively, the debt situation has improved. Consumer credit has quit growing. On a rate-of-change basis, debt has been coming down. Indebtedness as a percent of personal disposable income is down a couple of points. During the past couple of years, consumers have become unnerved and have been paying down indebtedness. Certainly not to where it was 10 or 15 years

ago, but the trend is there. Growth in personal income would allow some leeway to reduce paying down the indebtedness and put a little money into conspicuous consumption. In the consumer balance sheets of the 1980s, consumers' assets—physical and financial—went up about three-and-a-half times the amount of debt. Although debt did go up to an unnerving level for many people, based on a balance sheet approach, the consumer still has the wherewithal to spend. Both the indebtedness picture and the balance sheet analysis show improvement. Even after the buildup of debt in the 1980s, relative to their assets, consumers have the ability to start consuming enough to support the economic recovery.

The qualitative answer is even more bullish, and this is pure liberal arts economics; in other words, I am making a judgment about how human beings function. The human being has come through a learning process with respect to debt. Some anecdotal stories in the *Wall Street Journal* swear that people are lying awake at night worrying about how they are going to pay their bills and are telling other stories of personal anguish. Apart from conjectural possibilities, corporations and individuals have learned something from the 1990–91 recession. They have learned that taking on debt is a psychologically unpleasant experience. For some who have declared bankruptcy, it is a very tangibly unpleasant experience. From this learning experience will emerge a positive type of pro-savings, pro-investment economic behavior in the 1990s. This is one of the behavioral aspects of the argument for looking toward capital goods stocks and away from consumer stocks. The government, of course, is an entity unto itself that may have to be dealt with eventually.

Question: Is the current market mistaken in its pattern of valuation, or is it telling us something about the outlook for the recovery that may be different from what we have been expecting up until now?

Bostian: We are seeing a group or herd phenomenon in the mar-ket today. Maybe it is a little harsh to relate it to the nifty-fifty syndrome in the late 1960s and early 1970s, when "one-decision" stocks were selling at 40 times earnings. Some of those stocks did not have earnings-per-share growth rates in the top 100 on the New York Stock Exchange for the previous five years. Many established institutional portfolio managers were plowing money into their winners. One can argue about whether investors believed in the validity of that money flow or whether they just wanted to keep the game going without much thinking.

I do not think the consumer sector is dead, although the recent personal income and personal spending figures show some evidence of this. The consumer goods stocks, however, price a level of consumer buoyancy into them that is unrealistic. About two-thirds of that is blind market momentum, and maybe another third is a perception that these stocks have a second wind that comes from international markets opening up. The next big move is in the capital goods sector.

The Accuracy of Macroeconomic Forecasts

Stephen K. McNees
Vice President and Economist
Federal Reserve Bank of Boston

Macroeconomic forecasts have been more accurate in the past 10 years than they were in the 1970s. But now is not the time to become overly confident, because the tendency toward improvement might not continue.

In this presentation, I will address five questions relating to the accuracy of macroeconomic forecasts:

- Who is the best forecaster?
- How large are forecast errors?
- How have errors varied over time?
- Is forecast accuracy improving?
- What is the best forecasting technique?

Who Is the Best Forecaster?

Everybody wants to know who the best forecaster is. There isn't one. No one forecaster dominates for all or even most of the variables in which we are interested. Even for a specific variable, the ranking of the forecasters depends on such conditions as the horizon of the forecast, whether the forecast is of levels or of changes, and the exact concept that is of interest. (**Exhibit 1** contains a description of several prominent forecasting organizations.)

For example, suppose you want to find the best inflation forecaster. Looking over the track record of the past several years, Donald Ratajczak of Georgia State has the best record for the consumer price index (CPI) and for just about all time horizons. When inflation is measured by the implicit price deflator, however, other forecasters do better. Ratajczak is not the best forecaster of inflation of gross national product (GNP) prices. This is but one example in which, even with a specific question, the exact measure to be used makes a difference.

A forecaster's accuracy also depends on the type of forecast—that is, whether the forecast is of levels or of changes. **Table 1** presents the mean absolute errors of the forecasts of nominal GNP by levels and by changes. The *level* of GNP four quarters from now, at Q4, is the sum of the next four quarterly changes; the *change* at Q4 is from three quarters

ahead to four quarters ahead. A four-quarter-ahead forecast of nominal GNP is its annualized growth rate during the next four quarters. The levels version is cumulative; it includes the change in level in each preceding quarter. The change version estimates what the growth rate will be four quarters from now; for example, the growth rate in the first quarter of 1993 is a measure of the change from the last quarter of 1992. One measure is cumulative, and the other is quarter by quarter.

For changes in GNP, the Wharton Econometric Forecasting Associates forecast was more accurate in all but the one-quarter horizon. Wharton's record of accuracy in changes, however, does not make it the best at estimating the level of GNP, or the cumulative change. In this case, Data Resources, Inc., had the lowest error for levels at most time horizons.

The truth of the matter is that the forecasts of the prominent forecasters are very similar. Differences in accuracy are quite small, probably so small as to be insignificant in either the statistical or the economic sense. Not all forecasters are equally accurate, however; some are losers. You cannot pick a forecaster out of a hat, but the least accurate forecasters tend to drop out of the forecasting derby over time, which is one clear way to identify them.

How Large Are Forecast Errors?

The question of forecast errors is very important and largely neglected. Economists need to provide some measure of the reliability of their forecasts, or what some people call a confidence interval around the single point estimate of the forecast. This is not just an academic point. Business economists have had a hard time getting employment in the past decade because they have not spent enough time explaining

Exhibit 1. Summary Information on Forecasting Organizations

Forecasting Organization (Abbreviated Title), Contact for Further Information	Number of Macroeconomic Variables Forecast[a]	Typical Forecast Horizon, Quarters	Frequency of Release, per Year	Date Forecast First Issued Regularly
Benchmark Forecast (BMARK), George Washington University, Frederick Joutz, (202) 994-4899	30	8	4	1976
Data Resources, Inc. (DRI), Roger Brinner, (617) 863-5100	1,200	10 to 12	12	1969
Georgia State University (GSU), Economic Forecasting Project, Donald Ratajczak, (404) 651-3282	540	8	4	1973
Kent Economic and Development Institute, Inc. (KEDI), Vladimir Simunek, (216) 678-8215	1,700	10	12	1974
Laurence H. Meyer & Associates Ltd. (LHM), Larry Meyer, (314) 721-4747	450	7 to 11	12	1983
Research Seminar in Quantitative Economics (RSQE), University of Michigan, Saul Hymans, (313) 764-3299	200	8	8	1969
Survey of Professional Forecasters (SPF), Federal Reserve Bank of Philadelphia, formerly ASA/NBER, Dean Croushore, (215) 574-3809	20	5	4	1968
University of California at Los Angeles (UCLA), School of Business, David Hensley, (310) 825-1623	1,000	8 to 12	4	1968
Wharton Econometric Forecasting Associates, Inc. (WEFA), Kurt Karl, (215) 660-6357	1,000	12	12	1963

[a]Estimate.

Table 1. Mean Absolute Errors of Forecasts of Annual Growth Rates of Nominal GNP, 1Q1986–3Q1991
(percentage points)

Forecaster	Forecast Horizon							
	Q1	Q2	Q3	Q4	Q5	Q6	Q7	Q8
Levels								
BMARK	1.8	1.8	1.7	1.8	—	—	—	—
DRI	1.7	**1.3**	**1.3**	**1.2**	**1.2**	**1.1**	1.1	1.1
GSU	**1.6**	1.7	1.6	1.6	1.6	1.5	1.4	1.3
LHM	1.8	1.5	1.5	1.5	1.5	1.5	1.4	1.4
RSQE	2.1	1.6	1.5	1.4	1.3	**1.1**	**1.0**	—
WEFA	2.1	1.5	1.5	1.4	1.3	1.2	1.1	**1.0**
Changes								
BMARK	1.8	2.0	1.9	2.1	—	—	—	—
DRI	1.7	1.7	1.5	1.8	1.9	1.7	2.5	2.6
GSU	**1.6**	2.3	1.9	2.0	2.2	2.2	2.3	2.4
LHM	1.8	1.8	1.7	1.7	1.9	1.9	2.2	2.3
RSQE	2.1	1.8	1.7	1.7	1.7	1.8	2.2	—
WEFA	2.1	**1.6**	**1.4**	**1.6**	**1.6**	**1.5**	**1.8**	**2.2**

Source: Author's calculations based on data supplied by the forecasters.

Note: Numbers in boldface are smallest errors each quarter.

Key:
BMARK = Benchmark Forecast.
DRI = Data Resources, Inc.
GSU = Georgia State University.
LHM = Laurence H. Meyer & Associates Ltd.
RSQE = Research Seminar in Quantitative Economics.
WEFA = Wharton Econometric Forecasting Associates, Inc.

how much (or how little) they know and how much (or how little) confidence to place in their point estimate forecasts.

For example, forecast users would make a big mistake if they put equal weights on my forecasts of the exchange rate and the unemployment rate or my forecasts of the S&P 500 and the CPI. One of these forecasts is a wild guess; the other one will not be right on the nose, but it will be fairly close.

This need for confidence intervals, or measures of uncertainty, is so great that many people make the mistake of using the range of individual forecasts as a measure of the range of plausible outcomes. For example, a survey of what people think real growth will be in 1992 would probably show everybody estimating over 2 percent and nobody over 4 percent. That does not mean the probability is 100 percent that real growth will be between 2 percent and 4 percent. Far from it. A best guess as to the most likely outcome is quite different from the range of outcomes considered plausible. For example, I did a study a few years ago in which I compared the *Blue Chip* consensus forecast of seven different economic variables with the actual results.[1] Forty-four percent of

the actual outcomes fell outside the range of the *Blue Chip* forecasts—higher than the highest or lower than the lowest. Clearly, you always need to be aware of the consensus forecast, but you also need to pay attention to the outliers and the range of plausible outcomes.

The exact release date of an economic forecast is important as well. People are aware of the importance of timing in the financial markets, but timing is also important for quarterly economic variables such as real GNP.

The importance of timeliness is illustrated in **Figure 1**, which shows forecasts of the level of real GNP in a quarter by month of release. The quarter being forecasted would be T-3 to T-1. T is the date the first official estimate of the quarter becomes available. Little is known about actual GNP in a given quarter until the quarter actually begins. As the quarter starts and the high-frequency (daily, weekly, monthly) actual data roll in on that quarter, the learning curve—or the amount of error—goes down rapidly. To compare the accuracy of forecasts, they must have roughly similar release dates.

Whether a forecast is trying to predict a preliminary estimate or a final revision of actual data also makes a big difference. Typically, the actuals are revised more frequently for variables such as GNP

[1]Stephen K. McNees, "Consensus Forecasts: Tyranny of the Majority?" *New England Economic Review* (November/December 1987):15–21.

Figure 1. Trade-Off Between Timeliness and Reliability, Real GNP Estimates, 1Q1976–1Q1983

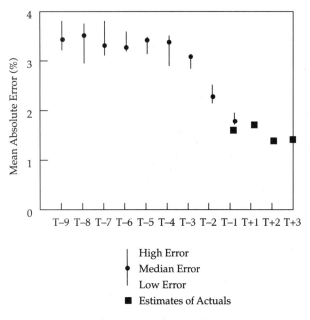

Source: Stephen K. McNees, "Estimating GNP: The Trade-Off Between Timeliness and Accuracy," *New England Economic Review* (January/February 1986):3–10.

Note: The forecasts are those of three of the most prominent commercial forecasting services.

than for financial data such as interest rates. The importance of the type of revision is illustrated in **Table 2**, which shows forecasts of real GNP growth rates one quarter ahead. The top portion judges accuracy relative to the preliminary data. The root mean squared error measures are about half as large for forecasts made late in the quarter as for forecasts made early in the quarter. Another interesting difference is that the outliers are much more dramatic for the early forecasts. For forecasts of preliminary data made in the first month of a quarter, 19 percent were more than 3 percentage points off the mark, whereas by the end of the quarter, only 1 percent were that far off, which probably means only one forecast. So, the process is a matter of ironing out the outliers as the high-frequency information comes in.

The bottom portion shows the accuracy of the same forecast relative to the revised estimate of the actual data for real GNP growth. The forecasters came much closer to the preliminary estimate than to the revised numbers because they have much of the same information that the Bureau of Economic Analysis (BEA) has when it makes its preliminary estimate. Neither the forecasters nor BEA has the information set that will be available two or three years later, when BEA makes its final revision.

The set of actuals used to judge forecast accuracy depends on how the forecast is going to be used. If forecasts are used to place a bet on the market reaction to data release, then the preliminary data are important. The revised data are more important to most people in nonfinancial corporations and to policymakers because their goal is to forecast what really happened. The difference between the two data sets is not trivial: The average revision in these growth rates during the 1970–91 period was 1.5 percentage points.

How Have Errors Varied Over Time?

The most important factor underlying the variability of forecast errors, the most important thing to define before measuring a forecast error, is the forecast period itself. The most interesting thing in forecasting accuracy is its variation over time, not who made the forecast or its release date.

Figure 2 is a time series of one-quarter-ahead forecast errors of real GNP. At first glance, the errors seemed to be all over the place, with no discernible pattern. In 1979 and 1980, however, the errors are quite dramatic. For six quarters in a row, virtually all forecasts of real GNP had the wrong sign. When-

Table 2. Forecast Errors, Current Quarter, Annual Growth Rates of Real GNP, 3Q1970–3Q1991

Item	Early (First month of quarter)	Late (Last month of quarter)
Preliminary actual data (percent of forecasts)		
> 1	65%	34%
> 2	29	11
> 3	19	1
Maximum error	7.4 points	3.8 points
Mean absolute error	1.9 points	0.9 points
Root mean squared error	2.5 points	1.2 points
Relative to revised actual data (percent of forecasts)		
> 1	72%	67%
> 2	48	31
> 3	32	19
Maximum error	10.9 points	4.9 points
Mean absolute error	2.4 points	1.7 points
Root mean squared error	3.1 points	2.1 points

Source: Author's estimates based on data from U.S. Bureau of Economic Analysis and data supplied by forecasters.

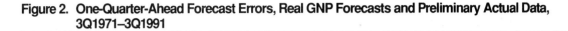

Figure 2. One-Quarter-Ahead Forecast Errors, Real GNP Forecasts and Preliminary Actual Data, 3Q1971–3Q1991

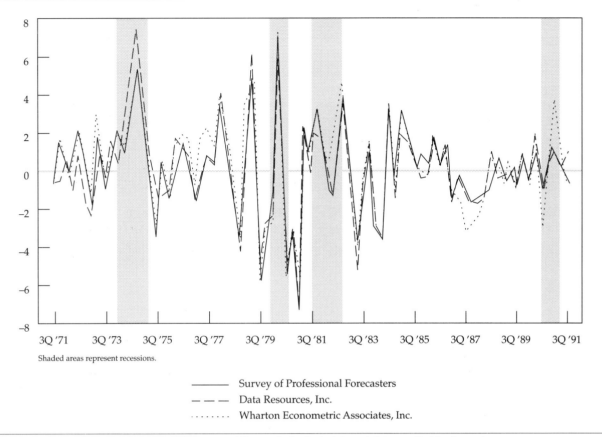

Shaded areas represent recessions.

——————— Survey of Professional Forecasters
— — — Data Resources, Inc.
· · · · · · · · Wharton Econometric Associates, Inc.

Source: Author's calculations based on U.S. Bureau of Economic Analysis data and data supplied by forecasters.

Note: The error is the predicted rate of growth less the BEA preliminary actual rate of growth.

ever we said GNP would go up, it went down, and vice versa. This occurred for longer than a year and was probably the low point in the prestige of economic forecasting. The only quarter for which we got the sign of real GNP right was the second quarter of 1980, when credit controls were imposed. Even then, the magnitude of the error was extremely large.

Nonfinancial corporations and policymakers must look at time spans longer than one quarter. Given the lag in monetary policy, whatever happens in the current quarter is essentially history. **Figure 3** shows the accuracy of four-quarter-ahead real GNP forecasts. Notice that the forecasts for the 1979–80 period, when all forecasters were hiding in disgrace, were not that bad. In both years, a big negative second quarter, which no one expected, was followed by a big positive third quarter no one expected. For the year as a whole, these large mistakes canceled out, and the forecasts were fairly accurate. The four-quarter-ahead forecasts did have two outstanding errors. One was the fiasco in 1974 caused by the dismantling of wage and price controls, an oil shock, a world commodity price explosion, and several other developments; the other was the error associated with the recession in 1982. The remaining years show some variations—some positive, some negative—but the most dramatic errors centered on those two major occasions.

The four-quarter-ahead forecasts of the GNP deflator, seen in **Figure 4**, were more accurate. Some significant underestimates were made in the 1970s, especially in the 1973–74 period. A similar underestimate occurred in 1978 and 1979, when another oil shock and unusual micro cost pressures raised the rate of inflation. Until the early 1980s, forecasters always underestimated the rate of inflation. That period was followed by one in which forecasters consistently overestimated inflation, particularly during the 1981–82 recession. Because no one expected that recession to be that bad, no one expected the degree of price deceleration we experienced. Since 1982, the range of error has been only about 1.5 percentage points up or down, and no particular tendency to over- or underestimate is evident.

Figure 3. Four-Quarter-Ahead Forecast Errors, Real GNP Forecasts and Preliminary Actual Data, 3Q1971–3Q1991

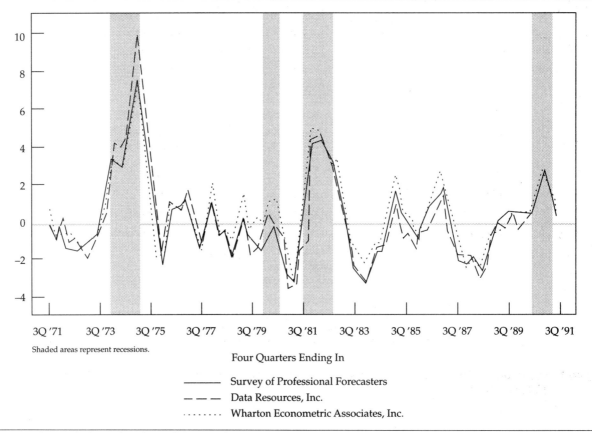

Shaded areas represent recessions.

Four Quarters Ending In

———— Survey of Professional Forecasters
— — — Data Resources, Inc.
· · · · · · · Wharton Econometric Associates, Inc.

Source: Author's calculations based on U.S. Bureau of Economic Analysis data and data supplied by forecasters.

Is Forecast Accuracy Improving?

Answering this question scientifically requires a much longer historical perspective. The longest continuous economic forecast series is the real GNP forecast made by the University of Michigan. Every November since 1952, the Research Seminar in Quantitative Economics has met in Ann Arbor to forecast real GNP.

The accuracy of the Michigan forecasts is shown in **Table 3**. The root mean squared error was lower in the 1960s than in the 1950s, and that for the 1980s was better than for the 1970s. The improvement over time is not unambiguous, however: The 1970s look worse than the 1960s. The far right column of Table 3 normalizes the root mean squared errors by expressing them as a ratio to the standard deviation of the actual real GNP. If real GNP has more variability, the standard errors will be bigger and the ratio will be smaller. The standard deviation of actual real growth in this case is an interesting number, because it would be the root mean squared error if the mean value of real GNP growth in the forecast period were forecasted precisely.

In the 1950s, the root mean squared error of Michigan's forecasts was almost as large as the standard deviation of actual GNP; the ratio was almost 1. The ratio went way down in the 1970s because the variability of actual GNP went up so much, and the ratio went down one more step in the 1980s. At least according to this one measure, the tendency toward improvement in forecasting accuracy is fairly clear.

This trend toward greater accuracy is not an iron law. Further improvement in the 1990s is not guaranteed. The competition is a constant race between improvements in forecasting techniques and changes in the structure of the economy itself. One area in which forecasting has improved is energy. When the first oil shock hit in 1973, we knew something about the direction or the sign of the resulting change in GNP, but we were almost at a loss concerning the amount of change, as shown by the large forecast errors during that period. Now, energy prices change by almost as much as they did in 1973, but the accuracy of the forecast is much better, particularly once the event has happened.

Another improvement is in the quantity of the data. In the 1950s and the 1960s, not a lot of good

Table 3. Accuracy of Real GNP Forecasts by the Research Seminar in Quantitative Economics, 1953–91

Years	Percentage Point Error			Ratio		
	ME	MAE	RMSE	MAE/N4	RMSE/SD	Actual
All	–0.1	1.3	2.0	0.51	0.70	
1953–71	–0.8	1.4	2.2		0.62	0.84
1972–91	0.5	1.2	1.6		0.43	0.57
1950–59	–1.5	2.1	3.2		0.59	0.90
1960–69	–0.7	1.0	1.4		0.71	0.85
1970–79	0.6	1.4	1.9		0.39	0.55
1980–89	0.2	0.9	1.3		0.44	0.51

Source: Based on forecasts by the Research Seminar in Quantitative Economics, University of Michigan, *The Economic Outlook for 1992*, Table 1, p. 4.

Key:
ME = mean error.
MAE = mean absolute error.
RMSE = root mean squared error.
N4 = naive "same as four-year average" forecast.
SD Actual = standard deviation of actuals in forecast period.

Figure 4. Four-Quarter-Ahead Forecast Errors, GNP Deflator Forecasts and Preliminary Actual Data, 3Q1971–3Q1991

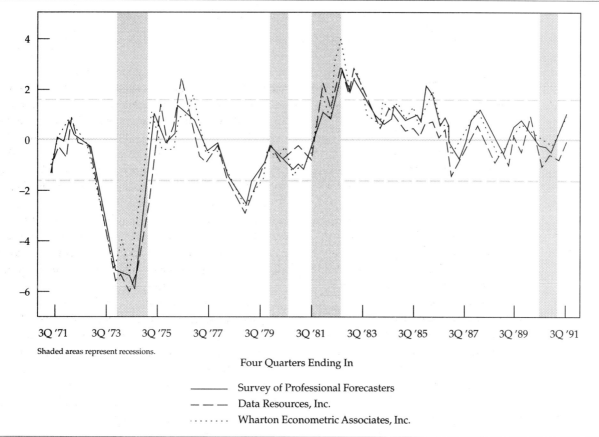

Shaded areas represent recessions.

Four Quarters Ending In

——— Survey of Professional Forecasters
– – – Data Resources, Inc.
· · · · · · · Wharton Econometric Associates, Inc.

Source: Author's calculations based on U.S. Bureau of Economic Analysis data and data supplied by forecasters.

forecasting data were available—particularly on recessions. In subsequent years, we have had eight or nine recessions, and we are beginning to learn more about what a recession is and what it could be. The amount of data we analyze, particularly quarterly data, is much larger than it was 10 or 20 years ago. In some other areas, the changes in the financial structure are so large and so frequent that any gains in accuracy are not obvious; in fact, we may be falling behind. Whether the gradual improvement in forecasts will be maintained remains to be seen.

What Is the Best Forecasting Technique?

The best forecasting technique is a blend of model and judgment, but not necessarily for financial variables. Many studies have shown that naive models are difficult, if not impossible, to beat for variables such as interest rates, stock market prices, and exchange rates. In contrast, for macroeconomic variables—including unemployment, real GNP, and the CPI—for which having a forecast that differs from the actual value does not create a profitable trading opportunity, simple rules of thumb or even complicated ARIMA- and VAR-type statistical models are fairly easy to beat.

Forecasters have much to be humble about. For these macro variables, the glass can be viewed as half full or half empty. The prominent forecasters beat any type of statistical rule of thumb for most macro variables, but the margin of superiority is disappointingly small. Coming within tenths of a percentage point on the growth rates presents an advantage, however. A model helps. Thinking helps. Judgment helps. All of those things help, but they do not make the difference between night and day. If you are Alan Greenspan, the ability to shave a few tenths off your forecasting error probably matters. For most people, however, whether the change in the CPI comes in at 4 percent or 3.75 percent does not matter much.

Conclusion

I used to say, "Forecasting accuracy has improved, but wait until the next turning point, the next business cycle, or the next recession!" Adding the 1990–91 recession to the data shows that forecasters were fairly late in recognizing the onset of this recession, but the magnitude of the errors in this period does not stand out; there was no spike, as in the 1970s.

For the past 10 years, macro forecasts have been more accurate than they were in the 1970s and probably more accurate than they were in the 1950s and the 1960s. Now is not the time to become overly confident, however. The tendency toward improvement may not continue. We need to be constantly alert to the possibility that we could have some huge, outlier horror stories, as we did in the 1950s and the 1970s.

Question and Answer Session

Stephen K. McNees

Question: Having 44 percent of the outcomes outside the range of the forecasts is disturbing. How do people who use this material deal with that? How seriously can forecasting be taken if that happens?

McNees: The only thing worse than a poor forecast is the misconception that you can operate without any coherent forecast or plan of what the future might bring. Most forecasters look at the same data, read the same newspapers, and use roughly similar approaches, despite their attempts to distinguish themselves. This implies that their best guesses will cluster fairly closely together. We usually need not only a "best guess" but also some idea of its reliability. We need to remember we would get different answers if we asked each individual to give not only their best guess but also the highest and lowest values they would find plausible.

Question: Most forecast errors are around turning points, when analysts need accuracy most. How does a consumer of this material deal with that situation?

Obviously, the consumer is likely to make the same kind of error. How do you try to second-guess this?

McNees: To some extent, you deal with turning points by looking at root mean squared errors instead of mean absolute errors. You could look at how somebody did at cyclical turning points and throughout the rest of the period, but I would be a little reluctant to do that. Penalizing large errors is probably the way to do it; look into accuracy. In a review of postwar recessions, I found that those recessions are usually accompanied by some "noneconomic" event.[2] Something strange is almost always going on at the time, usually something without a close historical precedent. The first oil shock was a good example. People did not even know how many gallons are in a barrel of oil, but they were trying to predict the impact of a quadrupling of the price of oil on the economy. The combination of big forecast

---

[2]Stephen K. McNees, "The 1990–91 Recession in Historical Perspective," *New England Economic Review* (January/February 1992):3–22.

errors and extraordinary economic events is probably unavoidable.

Question: How do you feel about the raw data you use?

McNees: I support the efforts to improve the quality of the data and the collection efforts. This is money well spent, because the result is socially positive. We all benefit from having better data and better forecasts. I do not want to diminish that effort. Some forecasters excuse their inaccurate forecasts on grounds of bad data. I was almost assaulted once at a meeting of forecasters back when we used to have the flash estimate of GNP. People said, "That estimate is garbage! It is worse than having nothing." I found that the flash was as accurate for real GNP as the estimate we now get 15 days after the quarter has ended. We privatized the flash. Now you pay to learn it instead of having the government provide it. I would be in favor of reinstating an early GNP report. Compared to other points in our history and to other countries, our data system is relatively good.

From Forecast to Portfolio Construction

Peter L. Bernstein
President
Peter L. Bernstein, Inc.

Because the objective in going from forecast to portfolio construction is to compose a set of assets with low covariance—to reduce risk while sustaining expected return—financial analysts must try to understand what makes the coefficient of correlation itself so variable. Sensitivity to paradigm shifts might well be the most important tool.

One of the most important questions in investment management is this: Why go from forecast to portfolio construction? A portfolio is several investments consisting of more than one asset. Today, we usually extend the meaning to denote several investments consisting of more than one asset *class*. "More than one" are the operative words. Thus, the question becomes this: Why is it necessary to hold more than one stock or more than one asset class?

The answer seems obvious. In an uncertain world, we are reluctant to put all our eggs in one basket. Yet no one ever thought systematically about this question until Harry Markowitz, as a graduate student at the University of Chicago, tackled it 40 years ago. Even then, for another 20 years, few practitioners paid any attention.

The whole revelation developed as a coincidence. Markowitz was not interested in finance but rather in linear programming, which is a sophisticated way of calculating the trade-offs that require us to sacrifice part of one thing if we want more of another. He thought investing might be an interesting application for linear programming, but he knew little about the subject.

The dean of the business school had Markowitz read John Burr Williams's classic, *The Theory of Investment Value*, which is the source of the dividend discount model.[1] Williams states at the outset of his book that the investor should buy "the best at the price." Markowitz observed, however, that investors do not buy "the best at the price." They diversify. The central point of Markowitz's analysis is that investors diversify because a portfolio behaves differently from a single asset. About choosing more

than one asset, Markowitz said:

$$VAR(r_p) = [X_1^2 * VAR(r_1)] + [X_2^2 * VAR(r_2)] + [2 * X_1 * X_2 * COV(r_1 r_2)].$$

Translated, this equation says the variability of a portfolio's rate of return—in this case, a two-asset portfolio—will be a function of three factors: the weight each asset carries in the portfolio, the variability of each asset, and the covariance between them. The weights, signified by X, are squared, meaning that weighting is important, which makes sense intuitively.

The most important part of the equation is the last expression, which says the variability is also dependent on the degree to which the assets move up and down together. Diversification serves no purpose if two assets move up and down together in perfect tandem. Then, holding the one with the lower expected return makes no sense.

The concept goes further than that. Diversification does not disturb the returns expected from an asset, but it does reduce risk. Thus, Markowitz's insight is significant: If you can reduce risk without reducing your expected return, your investments will be much more efficient than if you put all your eggs in one basket.

Diversification means hedging, and hedging means that one asset will go up as the other goes down. If that is not the case, you are not hedged. You are merely reducing expected return. A former colleague used to say that you are never truly diversified unless you own things you hate to hold. You expect them to do badly, but those are precisely the holdings that will come to your aid when the things you love to own turn out to be disasters.

---

[1] John Burr Williams, *The Theory of Investment Value* (Cambridge, Mass.: Harvard University Press, 1938).

The Message in the Capital Market Line

Going from forecast to portfolio construction begins with the capital market line, which tells us something about the trade-offs between risk and return. The evidence seems to confirm the basic principle that you cannot get rich by rolling over Treasury bills, but the variability of high-return assets is so high that you could end up broke by trying to get rich. The record also shows that some assets on occasion, such as long-term bonds and small-capitalization stocks, may provide returns too small relative to the risks involved in owning them. Intermediate-term bonds have been an anomaly that may offer a return premium relative to the risks they impose.

From 1925 to 1991, a portfolio of 60 percent S&P 500 and 40 percent long-term bonds fell above the capital market line and offered a return premium relative to the risk imposed (**Figure 1**). The return was equal to 60 percent of equity returns plus 40 percent of bond returns, but the variability was less than 60 percent of equity variability plus 40 percent of bond variability. This return premium has not been visible since the end of 1979, when the 60/40 portfolio slipped slightly below the capital market line (**Figure 2**). The risk turned out to be *more* than 60 percent of equity risk plus 40 percent of bond risk.

This change has two explanations. The obvious one is that bonds were a bad investment. Even though their returns were the highest they had been for any decade in recorded U.S. capital market history, they also had became much more volatile; even those huge returns were insufficient to compensate for the extraordinary increase in risk.

The less obvious explanation for the deterioration in the performance of the 60/40 portfolio was an upward shift in covariance. In the old days, stocks and bonds frequently moved in opposite directions. When business was good, stocks went up and bonds went down; when business was poor, the opposite happened. As bond yields increased over time, however, the competition from high interest rates began affecting stock behavior, and the correlation between stock and bond returns steadily rose. The coefficient of correlation from 1926 to 1956 was only 0.13; from 1956 to 1979, it was 0.29; but from 1980 to 1991, it was 0.39. Actually, it was much higher most of the time, except for 1974 and 1987, when stocks crashed and the bond market's move was more muted. In other words, the benefits of diversification diminished after 1979. With the two assets moving together most of the time, adding bonds to an all-equity portfolio reduced return proportionately more than it reduced risk.

The events of that period are dramatic, but they suggest an important generalization. If two assets are moving up and down together, why own the one with the lower expected return? When the coefficient of correlation between stock and bond returns is high, bonds should be excluded from the portfolio. They are attractive only when we expect them to provide positive returns at times when the stock market is weak.

Can We Forecast the Covariance?

If the objective in going from forecast to portfolio construction is to compose a set of assets with low covariance—to reduce risk while sustaining expected return—then we must try to understand what makes the coefficient of correlation itself so variable.

Diversification improves the efficiency of investing. The critical difference between stocks and bonds is the variability of the fundamental determinants of their values—their expected cash flows. Bonds are contracts to pay their owners a predetermined flow of nominal cash payments over a period of time. Expected cash flows from bonds are uncertain only

Figure 1. The Capital Market Line, 4Q1925–4Q1991

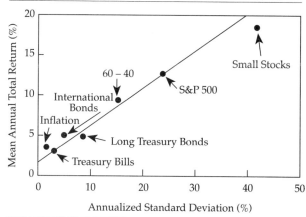

Source: Ibbotson Associates.

Figure 2. The Capital Market Line, 4Q1979–4Q1991

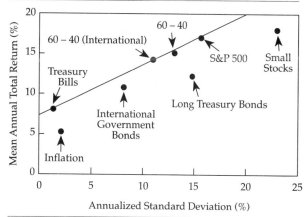

Source: Ibbotson Associates.

when the borrower's solvency is open to question. Nothing, however, is predetermined about the cash flows from equities. They are variable and, therefore, uncertain. Also, no prescribed time period will terminate their expected cash flows.

These observations apply to the nominal cash flows from each asset, which may differ from the real purchasing power of that money. The real value of nominally fixed cash flows from bonds is highly uncertain because inflation is highly uncertain. Real cash flows from equities are also uncertain, but less so because they are a claim on cash flows that depend on the nominal volume of business activity.

These obvious distinctions provide important insights into the tendencies of stock and bond prices to move together or in opposite directions. The correlation is high when stocks acquire bondlike characteristics or when bonds acquire stocklike characteristics.

Stocks are bondlike when corporations are unable to pass inflation through to the bottom line, and real earnings and dividends lag behind the inflation rate. Expected equity cash flows then take on a family resemblance to the fixed flows from bonds, which always lag behind the inflation rate.

Bonds are stocklike when borrowers flirt with bankruptcy so that the viability of the contracts underlying their cash flows becomes questionable. Consequently, junk bonds have a higher correlation with stocks than with high-grade bonds, and they frequently do well in booming business conditions, even though interest rates are rising.

A second—and partly related—feature of equities also distinguishes them from bonds: growth. Bond coupons are always the same amount, whereas dividends can increase. The more likely they are to increase, especially relative to inflation, the more likely stocks will move independently of the bond market. If dividend growth is perceived as sluggish, however, and dividend payments begin to look like bond coupons, the correlation between the two asset classes should rise (**Figure 3**).

A Correlation Model

To examine the stock/bond correlation further, I developed a model in which the coefficient of correlation is determined by the year-over-year rate of growth in real dividends and by the spread between corporate return on investment (ROI) and the growth rate of employee compensation. This second variable is a proxy for how successfully the corporation passes inflation through to the bottom line.

I estimated the model for the 1979–89 time period. Because ROI data are annual, I estimated the

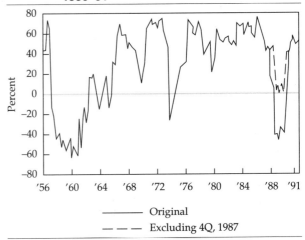

Figure 3. Coefficient of Correlation Between Bond and Stock Returns over 10 Quarters, 1956–91

——— Original
– – – Excluding 4Q, 1987

Source: Ibbotson Associates.

Note: Data based on returns for Standard & Poor's 500 and U.S. Treasury bonds.

model over full-year periods, which provides only a small number of data points. The coefficients of correlation are annual averages of running 10-quarter correlations. The results are shown in **Figure 4**.

The model confirms that the correlation between stock and bond returns is high when the spread between ROI and employee compensation narrows, and it is low when the corporation's inflation pass-through is strong. The correlation is also high when real dividend growth is sluggish and low when real dividend growth is vigorous. Together, the two variables explain more than 60 percent of the variability of the coefficient of correlation. ROI minus compensation, on its own, has an R^2 of 0.38; the dividend-growth variable has an R^2 of 0.47.[2]

The model shows that, since 1959, investors paid little attention to bond/stock correlations during the years before inflation worries set in about 1965 or 1966. Until that time, the coefficient of correlation was on the negative side because few people questioned the ability of corporations to hedge inflation. Also, growth was beginning to replace the Graham and Dodd valuation as the driving concept in stock selection.

The model came into its own during the 1970s and 1980s because interest rates rose enough to become significant. The fourth quarter of 1987 is excluded from the calculations because it would have pulled the volatility estimate for that year way out of line and limited the model's applicability. I do show

---

[2]Because the two independent variables are closely correlated, the R^2 of the model may be biased upward by perhaps 10 basis points.

Figure 4. Coefficient of Correlation Between Bond and Stock Returns, Actual and Fitted, 1959–91

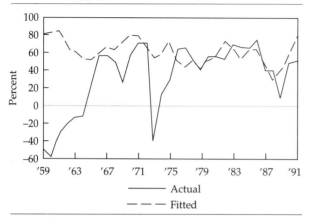

—— Actual

– – – Fitted

Sources: Ibbotson Associates, Standard & Poor's, and the Bureau of Labor Statistics.

Note: Data exclude fourth quarter of 1987.

the distortion of 1973 and 1974, which is not included in the estimation period for the model.

Declining dividend growth rates and poor profitability produced a 1991 estimate of 0.80 percent, one of the highest coefficients in this 22-year history. The actual coefficient of about 0.50 percent is well below 0.80 percent and below the average of the past 15 years. This estimation error suggests two possibilities. First, the parameters may have shifted, so the model estimated from 1979 to 1989 no longer applies. I doubt that, however, because nothing has happened to change investor perceptions of the roles of stocks and bonds in their portfolios. Second, and more likely, the error is a consequence of the recession. In that case, the error will shortly correct itself either by a rising correlation between stock and bond returns, so that the actual advances meet the estimate, or by an acceleration in dividend growth and better profitability, in which case the estimate drops to meet the actual. My own sense of the matter favors the latter possibility, with ROI minus compensation improving in 1992 and dividend growth following suit in 1993.

How Much Bang for the Buck?

Another route from forecast to portfolio construction is through the expected equity risk premium, or the excess return of equities over bond returns. The major quantitative tactical asset allocation organizations focus on the spread in the expected returns between equities and bonds, or among equities, bonds, and cash. If the spread is wider than normal, buy stocks and sell bonds. If equities are expected to

outperform bonds by a smaller amount than usual, sell stocks and buy bonds.

The trick is to define "normal." Some asset allocators consider the long-term mean to be the norm. Some organizations, such as Wells Fargo and Mellon, insist that adding bells and whistles contributes nothing to forecast accuracy. Others, such as First Quadrant and TSA Capital Management, consider a moving target normal and add extra variables such as economic data, market sentiment figures, and price momentum to indicate what the spread should be at any given moment.

One bell (or is it a whistle?) appeals to me because it has received little or no attention and the underlying rationale makes intuitive sense. History shows that the equity risk premium is larger when real returns on bonds are poor, rather than when real returns on bonds are high (**Figure 5**).

The great periods for the equity risk premium, such as the great bull market of the late 1940s to the late 1960s, built up when the bond market's performance was pathetic. A similar pattern is visible between the discovery of gold at the end of the 19th century and the end of World War I. For some extended periods of time, equity risk premiums were either zero or negligible, and bonds were earning good real returns during all those periods.

The explanation for this phenomenon is simple. Real returns on high-grade bonds are systematically related to inflation. Real returns are good when inflation is low or deflation prevails; real returns are poor when the price level is rising rapidly. Once again, stocks are different. They have no consistent

Figure 5. Nominal Risk Premium on Stocks Versus Real Bond Return, 1801–1991

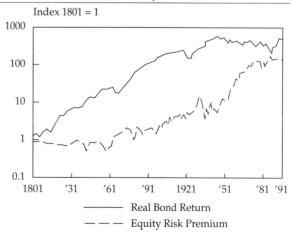

—— Real Bond Return

– – – Equity Risk Premium

Source: Jeremy Siegel, Wharton School, University of Pennsylvania.

Note: Risk premium equals equity return minus nominal bond return.

relationship to inflation and deflation, and they have done well and poorly under both scenarios.

The relationship between the equity risk premium and real bond returns arises from this dichotomy. Real bond returns are a function of inflation, pure and simple. Stocks do what they are going to do regardless, but they usually go up. As a result, they outperform bonds significantly when bonds do badly and outperform only slightly when bonds do well. The relationship is not perfect because stocks do not go up *all* the time or at a constant rate, but the relationship does explain why the return premium on equities was so large during periods such as 1900 to 1921 or the great inflation from the mid-1960s through the 1970s. It also explains why the narrow spread between stock and bond returns during the disinflationary 1980s should not have been surprising.

Volatility is another feature of market behavior that deserves attention. Volatility is a good proxy for risk because it means future wealth levels are uncertain. If the volatility of one asset rises relative to another, the asset with increased volatility should require a higher return.

The changes in the relative volatility of stocks and bonds tend to lead the spread between bond yields and the dividend yield on stocks, which in turn are proxies for their expected returns. This phenomenon was most striking in the early 1980s, when bonds became far more volatile than they had ever been. Bond yields went through the roof, but equity yields rose by only a couple of percentage points, pushing the yield spread to record heights. In contrast, from 1973 to 1976, the yield spread narrowed by about 200 basis points as stocks showed the highest volatility since the 1930s (**Figure 6**).

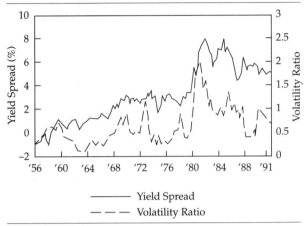

Figure 6. Bond Yield Minus Stock Yield Versus Ratio of Bond Volatility to Stock Volatility, 1956–91

Sources: Ibbotson Associates, Standard & Poor's.

Note: Volatility measured over 10 quarters.

The Most Important Tool

These propositions look good on the charts. Good ideas appear to produce good results, especially when they rest on fundamental economic principles, commonsense concepts, and theories of how human beings behave. Yet the major lesson of financial history is the instability of most relationships. The theories still hold, but the importance of one factor zooms upward and another sinks into insignificance. Theory can explain many of these shifts after the fact, but theory does not tell us when the parameters are about to burst apart.

My strongest conviction about the whole issue of moving from forecast to portfolio is that sensitivity to paradigm shifts is the most important tool. All models and assumptions must be tested with great frequency. Only then can theory be comfortably blended with practice.

Question and Answer Session

Peter L. Bernstein

Question: How accurately can covariances be predicted relative to total variances?

Bernstein: Total variances usually are not hard to predict because the volatility of any given asset does not have that much variability. Then, we think of what happened to bonds in the early 1980s or the stock market in the fall of 1987, so asset variability is not easy to predict either. By itself, bond volatility is much easier to predict than stock volatility because it is closely related to what happens to inflation. Another important element of bond volatility is that we use the standard deviation as a handy measure of variability. We less often use the coefficient of variation, which is the standard deviation divided by the mean. In other words, the measure is standardized, so if something has a mean of 80 and a standard deviation of 20 and another has a mean of 10 and a standard deviation of 20, clearly the standard deviation of 20 in the second case is more meaningful than that in the first case.

If we look at the history of bond market volatility from the 1950s through 1981, bonds became volatile far beyond any earlier period in history. We forget, however, that interest rates were also far higher than in any earlier period in history. So the coefficient of variation of bond returns was not that high in the early 1980s. Actually, it was higher in the early 1970s. Bonds were more volatile relative to their level of interest rates in the early 1970s than in the 1980s. Nothing unusual is happening relative to history.

Stock market volatility is a function of how we feel about the whole economic system. In the 1930s, stock market volatility was entirely different from any other period of U.S. stock market history. In the 1930s, people could not take a long-term view. They did not know whether this system was going to survive. It was a period when time horizons were very blurry. Uncertainty will affect stock market volatility. By and large, whatever the Ibbotson–Sinquefield standard deviation number is, sometimes about 18 percent a year, it is a good number, and one I would stick with.

Question: Given that the Fed has resolved to prop up our financial system—no large banks can fail, easy money, and so forth—and given the proclivity of the federal government to rack up higher deficits, might inflation be more of a problem than is expected?

Bernstein: The case for low inflation during the 1990s has much going for it. One must be alert on two scores, however. The first involves the real economy: We do not have much slack as we come out of this recession. The recession has been long, nasty, and very bad in some places, but overall it has not been very deep. The unemployment rate is nowhere near as high as in earlier recessions. Capacity utilization is at 78 percent. I have good reason to support the statement that the official capacity figures are overstated. The 12 plants of General Motors are still in the numbers but will be going out. The overhead slack is low, and two years or so of 3 percent growth can be a bad kind of overheating, resulting in cost-push kinds of problems. All is not clear sailing on inflation.

The other thing farther out is the debt overhang problem, particularly public debt overhang. This has traditionally been solved by printing money and by impatience with other means of dealing with this problem. President Bush's budget message was the first in history that did not show revenue and expenses converging in the future. All of us knew that forecasts of such a convergence could not be taken very seriously, but at least where there is a will, there is a way. Now the will is gone. The problem of deficit reduction has been abandoned. These are not causes for concern in 1992, but they may be beginning in 1993 and definitely beyond that.

Question: If real yields stay high during the next several years, is this an argument against holding stocks in a portfolio, given the risk–reward trade-off your presentation implies?

Bernstein: Real returns should remain high, if you believe in the low-inflation case. Then the choice between stocks and bonds becomes difficult. Eight percent on bonds with inflation running between 3 and 4 percent is what a former partner of mine used to call a "good New England return." To a forecaster, a 4 percent real return makes bonds very attractive. Although stocks might do better, maybe earn a nominal 10 percent, a spread of 2 points given the difference of variability is not much. If you have concerns about inflation, then the whole thing becomes easier, because bond returns may still be real.

Bondholders will not go through that agony again. They have learned something. Bond returns may still be real, but they will not be 4 percent, and bonds may decline in price. In that case, stocks are more attractive, and the trade-off becomes easier. If you believe inflation is likely to be in the 3 to 4 percent range for a while, then the choice is much harder to make.

Constructing Fixed-Income Portfolios

Chris P. Dialynas
Managing Director
Pacific Investment Management Company

Portfolio managers use economic inputs to select securities that express their confidence in the macro inputs. Consequently, the relative volatility of a portfolio is a function of confidence in the inputs.

Portfolio management is a wonderful occupation. A portfolio manager is scientist, artist, psychologist, mathematician, political scientist, and more than anything else, economist—a jack-of-all-trades and master of some. Because bond portfolio managers must understand the dynamics of interest rate changes and successfully forecast those changes, they must understand economic forecasts in practical macroeconomic terms and then translate them into interest rate forecasts. Although knowing what gross domestic product (GDP) and inflation will be one quarter and one year forward is nice, knowing what the yield on 2-, 10-, and 30-year Treasury securities will be at the end of those periods is much more important.

Using Macroeconomic Forecasts

No simple, reliable rules exist for using economic inputs to arrive at an interest rate forecast. Some basic requisites can be identified, however. First, portfolio managers must understand, or create, the link between an economic forecast and an interest rate forecast. Normally—but not always—fast growth or high inflation means higher interest rates, and slow growth/low inflation means lower rates. Second, portfolio managers must be able to integrate a long-term, or secular, economic forecast with the shorter term cyclical forecast. Third, they must understand how a forecast affects the desirability of classes of bonds and individual bonds.

Portfolio managers must also understand that, because social, behavioral, and regulatory changes may alter the accepted relationships, the forecast inputs can be wrong. The proper interpretation of exogenous, unexpected shocks and their effect on the portfolio is necessary. Many such shocks have oc-curred in recent years. The stock market crash, the fall of the Berlin Wall, the war in the Persian Gulf, the banking crisis, and the turmoil in the former Soviet Union are but a few. Exogenous shocks can reinforce belief in a forecast or render it useless.

The belief at our firm is that understanding the elements of a forecast—the "why"—is just as important as understanding the forecast itself. For that reason, the firm has no economist *per se* but relies upon the collective wisdom of the investment professionals. We debate the theoretical and empirical issues to exhaustion. This is a difficult but productive process that helps in understanding the backbone of the forecast, the assumptions that underlie it, the dynamics of the elements upon which it is built, and the risks it might be wrong. We never leave a meeting certain that the forecast is correct.

Each topic discussed at these meetings develops into an input in the bond management process. These topics include housing activity, business investment, consumer spending, regulatory and tax policy prospects, international trade, Federal Reserve policy, fiscal policy, and political constraints, among others.

The number of equations embedded within an econometric forecasting model indicates the complexity of an economist's job. Econometric models often break down because structural, regulatory, or social changes affect the variables in unpredictable ways. Even portfolio managers who do not use econometric models in forecasting interest rates should be fully aware of their forecasts' conditionality and establish an appropriate level of confidence about them. High confidence justifies strong statements about the various portfolio themes. Low confidence requires weak, neutral, or hedged statements. Hedged statements, implemented with option strategies, can be powerful because a bias can be expressed and the downside risk limited. The portfolio manager's role is to assign probabilities to the inputs used in models to evaluate securities and strategies.

For bond managers, the most important macroeconomic forecast is the interest rate forecast, including long-term structure and a set of volatility assessments. Also important are forecasts of credit quality and capital structure trends, consumer spending, personal finance behavior, and the real and financial economics of other important countries.

The practical dimensions of bond management are illustrated in **Figure 1**. The goal for portfolio managers is to add value. Bond managers have many ways to accomplish this. The most potent method is usually the duration strategy, which is the implementation of an interest rate forecast. The second most important aspects of bond management are sector selection and the choice of the distribution of cash flows along the yield curve. Either can be as important as duration strategy, but they are usually secondary conditions. Both decisions are influenced by the substantive elements of the economic forecast.

Figure 1. Bond Portfolio Management Simplified

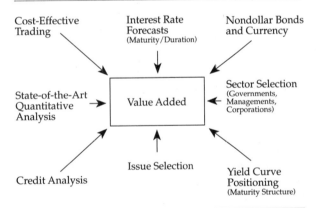

Source: Pacific Investment Management Co.

Under most circumstances, individual issue selection within a sector or subsector is relatively trivial. Of course, exceptions do occur on both the upside and the downside; these exceptions can usually be identified through rigorous credit or mortgage analysis. In practice, many methods can be used to add value—some more potent than others, but all dependent on a good set of inputs from the economic forecast.

All portfolio managers have a bias about the probability distribution of their forecasts, and they select securities for their portfolios based upon that bias. This appropriate behavior has important implications for the valuation of individual securities

and the portfolio. First, such behavior biases the distribution of expected interest rates and expectations about the forward shape of the yield curve. It may bias the portfolio's duration and the decision as to which particular securities a portfolio holds. The biases affect the risk–reward trade-offs associated with the usual assumption of "normal" return distributions. For bonds, these biases can be expressed in a strong form with call and put options. The strongest form of expression of these biases is probably through mortgage-related instruments when prepayment rate assumptions are incorporated into a strategy. These biases generally relate to confidence in the forecast and, in practice, are inputs into bond valuation models, which are generally constructed as risk-neutral, unbiased models. The strength of the biases is important to understand, even if the biases are intentional.

Risk Measurement

Risk is of at least two types—absolute and relative. A bond portfolio's risk is expressed through several parameters: duration, convexity, sector distribution, yield curve distribution, and credit quality. Most often, an investment manager's performance is defined in relative terms; for bond people, that generally means relative to the Lehman Brothers Government/Corporate Bond Index or the Lehman Brothers Aggregate Index. **Table 1** compares the absolute characteristics of these indexes. Because few mortgages were below par at the end of 1991, the durations of these portfolios were substantially different. Also, because the convexity was heavily skewed toward the government/corporate index, both portfolios are high-quality bullets—that is, they contain a

Table 1. General Attributes of the Indexes (Bogeys), January 1992

Attribute	LBG/C[a]	Aggregate[b]
Duration	5.00	4.20
Convexity	Good	Poor
Sectors		
Government	76%	52%
Corporate	24	18
Mortgage		30
Yield curve		
Intermediate	68	78
Long term	32	22
Quality	AA	AA+

Source: Pacific Investment Management Co.

[a]Lehman Brothers Government/Corporate Bond Index.
[b]Lehman Brothers Aggregate Index.

large proportion of intermediate securities of high credit quality.

A bond portfolio may also include instruments that are not in the comparison index—nondollar bonds and high-yield bonds, for example. These introduce a new element into the traditional relative risk–reward framework. These two sectors are potent sources of return opportunity but should only be used when confidence in the sector forecast is high. They are, in essence, the strong-form expression of confidence in the macroeconomic inputs. In 1991, a 10 percent position of high-yield bonds in a portfolio would have provided value added in excess of 2 percent. The Federal Reserve bailout with its reliquification theme paid off nicely.

The simplest and oldest measures of risk are average maturity and average quality. Today, managers also look at historical standard deviation of return to measure the riskiness of a particular class of assets or a portfolio. **Figure 2** shows some measures of asset-class risk and how an optimal combination of unconstrained portfolio combinations of these asset classes can substantially alter a portfolio's risk–return character. A natural problem with historical data, however, is the misinformation that averaging can create.

Figure 2. Unconstrained Efficient Frontier with and without Hedged International Securities, 1978–91

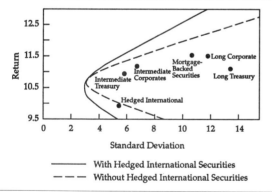

Source: Pacific Investment Management Co.

Portfolio duration is generally regarded as the supreme statement about investment-grade bond portfolio risk. **Figure 3** shows the potential deficiency, and deception, of duration as a risk measurement for bond portfolio management and performance standardization. The ultimate objective is to quantify the portfolio's expected risk—that is, its expected volatility. Historically, short-term interest rates are more volatile than long-term rates, which can distort the measurement of risk. A volatility-adjusted duration calculation, which incorporates in-

Figure 3. Duration and Adjusted Duration, Treasury Yield Curve, October 8, 1991

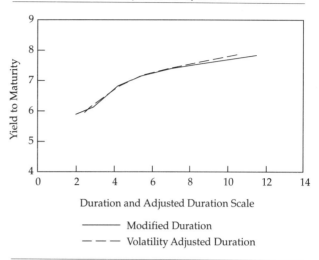

Source: Pacific Investment Management Co.

terest rate levels and expected interest rate volatility stemming from term structure, more accurately captures expected portfolio volatility than the usual duration measure. Figure 3 shows some volatility-adjusted durations and the nonlinear shrinking of conventional durations.

Figure 4 shows how holding portfolio duration constant produces different expected portfolio volatilities for different combinations of bonds. Given a duration target of five years, for example, a portfolio constructed of two-year securities leveraged up to the five-year duration target would have an expected standard deviation of 6 percent. The standard deviation of a 5-year-duration portfolio constructed with cash and 30-year bonds would be only 4.25 percent. The duration measurement suggests equal risk, but

Figure 4. Portfolio Volatility at Different Durations

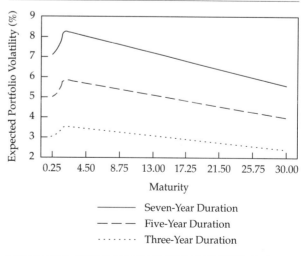

Source: Pacific Investment Management Co.

the volatility measurement suggests one portfolio contains 33 percent more risk than the other.

This portfolio management problem can be viewed another way. Once bond managers have determined a duration and yield curve strategy, they can measure a portfolio's riskiness relative to that of a bogey to understand the potency of the statement the portfolio is making.

Risk measurement of bond portfolios certainly needs more development; conventional measures have always been inadequate. We focus on risk because it represents a statement of conviction about our forecasts. A portfolio's volatility level depends upon duration, yield curve distribution, convexity, and quality (**Table 2**). The duration, yield curve, and volatility statements are outputs of the economic forecast and serve as inputs to the interest rate forecasting process. Once a portfolio is created and parametized in this fashion, the strength of conviction about the macroeconomic forecast should become apparent. This framework serves as a check between belief and reality. Also, it can be stated in relative parameters—that is, deviations from a bogey—and can be used to test convictions.

Table 2. Portfolio Character, Expected Volatility

Attribute	High	Low
Duration	Long	Short
Yield curve distribution	Bullet	Barbell
Convexity	Low	High
Quality	Low	High

Source: Pacific Investment Management Co.

Sector and Asset Selection

A detailed guide to bond portfolio management is shown in **Figure 5**. The figure demonstrates the importance of the qualitative elements of an interest rate forecast, such as expectations about housing, credit quality, robustness of growth, and volatility within the system, and the specific aspects of the forecast itself.

The inputs to the forecast are designated by arrows from the macroeconomic forecast to the functional elements: duration, prepay rates, quality, volatility, yield curve shape, and international bonds. Portfolio managers alter the probability distribution

Figure 5. Bond Portfolio Management Guide

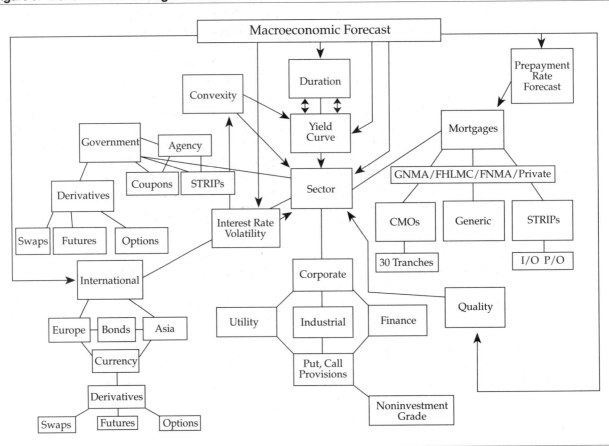

Source: Pacific Investment Management Co.

of these inputs based upon the strength of their convictions. Managers also must prioritize these elements, because a combination of forecasts may constrain actual bond selection. Suppose a manager believes that interest rates will drop across the yield curve but that the two-year rate will drop by more than the seven-year rate; of the two choices, the manager prefers the two-year part of the yield curve. The decision is unfulfilling because the duration objective is six years, which is longer than the bogey. Without leverage, these two objectives are mutually exclusive.

The yield curve strategy also affects sector choices, as does the basic macro forecast itself. Again, a manager must make trade-offs between perceptions of sector value and changes in yield curve shape. The choice is complicated further because changes in the yield curve shape can exert powerful effects on sector valuation through discount rate changes and their potential effect on economic activity. For example, a manager might think interest rates will fall and the yield curve will steepen because the Federal Reserve is in an aggressive easing mode. The manager believes the strategy will be successful, growth will result, and therefore, credit quality will improve. Quality spreads are wide, and the manager wants to increase his holdings. He chooses those with the most potential—long, noncallable industrials and banks. Once again, the greater expected value choice must be made.

An important macroeconomic variable to consider is expected volatility, which is a market-determined measure of the expected variability of various components of the term structure, the expected volatility of credit quality, and the expected variability of prepayment rates during the investment horizon, among other factors. Expected volatility is important because it is the key factor in the quantification of options. Most bonds have embedded options. Mortgages have prepayment options; corporates have credit quality as an option and may contain refunding options, sinking funds, or put options; futures contracts have quality and quantity options; and even government securities contain options because of their convexity characteristics. The practical importance of these options is that they affect the duration and yield of a security and, ultimately, its terminal investment horizon price.

The "volatility" input is used to select sectors and subsectors for investment. For example, a forecast of a stable credit situation, combined with a forecast for more stable interest rates, should lead an

investor into callable corporate bonds. The forecasted truncated volatility numbers are used to quantify the value of particular bonds within the sector.

A more stable international political/economic environment may lead an investor into nondollar bonds. A forecast for a more volatile interest rate environment and a stable yield curve shape may motivate an investor to create convex portfolios. The choice is not so simple, however. Changes in volatility expectations will affect the yield curve shape and must be incorporated into the decision-making process. The potential combinations of scenarios are limitless. This guide is merely a framework demonstrating the complexity of the process and the importance of the economic inputs to the selection of securities.

Table 3 is a simplified guide to asset selection. The column heads list the economic inputs, and the rows present growth and recession scenarios for corporate, mortgage-related, and government bonds. The body of the table shows particular types of bonds that normally fit the bill under the given circumstances. In the corporate sector, for example, the low-volatility/growth scenario suggests an investor might find value in low-quality, callable bonds. The intuition is quite simple. Growth provides for stable-to-improving credit quality, and the declining volatility of interest rates reduces the value of the call option the investor sells to the issuer on the corporate bond. In this example, the expectation is that the corporate/Treasury yield spread will contract.

For mortgages, under high-volatility/recession expectations, the table recommends convex interest-only (IO) STRIPS, discount FHA/VA project loans, and planned amortization class mortgages. The IOs are a strong statement about declining prepayment assumptions associated with a recessionary environment, and the other two security classes are weaker statements about the same input.

Conclusion

Table 3 is only a guide, which—when used with Figure 5—shows a structure for using economic inputs in the bond management process. Portfolio managers use the economic inputs to select sectors and securities that express their confidence in the macro inputs. The greater the confidence in the inputs, the more the portfolio will vary from the "bogey" portfolio. Consequently, the relative volatility of the portfolio will be a function of confidence in the inputs.

Table 3. Asset Selection Guide

Sector/Forecast	High Volatility	Low Volatility	Lower Rates, Steeper Yield Curve	Lower Rates, Flatter Yield Curve	Higher Rate, Steeper Yield Curve	Higher Rates, Flatter Yield Curve
Corporates						
Growth	Lower quality Noncallable	Lower quality Callable	Lower quality Noncallable	Lower quality Noncallable Putable	Lower quality Callable	Lower quality Putable Callable
Recession	Avoid	Higher quality Callable	Avoid	Avoid	Avoid	Avoid
Mortgage						
Growth	Convex PO Discount mortgages PACs	Premium PACs Nonagency Pass-throughs	Current coupon PO Long discount CMO	Current coupon PO Long Z tranches	Positively convex IO Premium pass-throughs	Avoid
Recession	Convex IO Discount projects PACs	Negative convex Pass-throughs Negative convex IO	Current coupon Pass-throughs Intermediate PACs	Long PACs	Positively convex IO Premium pass-throughs	Positively convex IO Premium pass-throughs
Governments						
Growth	Barbell	Bullet	Long bullet	Long barbell	Cash	Cash
Recession	Barbell	Bullet	Long bullet	Long barbell	Cash	Cash

Source: Pacific Investment Management Co.

PO = principal-only STRIPS.
PAC = planned amortization classes.
IO = interest-only STRIPS.
CMO = collateralized mortgage obligations.

Selecting Fixed-Income Securities

Robert W. Kopprasch, CFA
Senior Vice President
Alliance Capital Management L.P.

An alternative to traditional fixed-income portfolio management techniques involves outperforming benchmarks through sector and security selection rather than interest rate anticipation.

One obvious approach to fixed-income portfolio management is to estimate interest rate movements and then adjust the portfolio's duration accordingly. Unfortunately, most people cannot do that consistently. Another approach is to look for value in the marketplace, outperforming benchmarks through sector and security selection rather than interest rate anticipation.

At Alliance Capital Management, we characterize ourselves as value managers. We attempt to outperform fixed-income benchmarks through sector and security selection rather than through interest rate anticipation. Thus, the duration of our institutional portfolios is normally within six months of their benchmark durations. The particular structure through which we achieve that duration reflects our view of value across the yield curve and in different sectors.

Our firm's institutional fixed-income products include international, sector rotation, and mortgage strategies. The investment process is similar across disciplines, but each uses its own particular mix of economic inputs in the estimation of investment value. In this presentation, I will concentrate on the inputs used in managing mortgage-backed securities (MBS).

Each of our institutional disciplines attempts to discover value within the relevant sectors. For the international group, sector usually means "country" or "currency," and for sector rotation, the sectors are broadly defined as Treasuries, corporates, and mortgages. Within the mortgage strategies, the sector can be FHA/VA or conventional, discount versus premium, collateralized mortgage obligations (CMOs) or collateral, interest-only (IO) or principal-only (PO), and so forth. The approach is to look at housing fundamentals to determine the outlook for housing turnover and mortgage refinancing. As investors in a specific sector, we look at some data that are not normally examined.

Fundamental Analysis

The investment process for each of our fixed-income products starts with a weekly review of global interest rate trends. We use fundamental economic and market data to assess the probability of change in interest rates and interest rate volatility, major trends in global interest rates, term structures, and capital flows and relationships between domestic and international influences on volatility and rates. We also review how current actual and implied volatility levels may affect our portfolios, the optionality of certain instruments, and so on. The term structure is examined to gain information about market expectations and to select an optimum duration structure—for example, bullet versus barbell. Often, yield curve considerations lead us to look for attractive barbell structures. At other times, the barbell decision is determined by the perception of value in short- or long-duration instruments, which forces a barbell to achieve the desired portfolio duration.

We use fundamental and quantitative techniques to determine which sectors offer the greatest risk-adjusted returns. We review developments and expectations in nominal and option-adjusted spreads in Treasury, corporate, mortgage, and international sectors. These discussions are led by sector specialists and credit specialists. We have found with high-yield portfolios, for example, that having credit specialists on our staff is important. We now have 10 professionals in fixed-income research, and this expansion represents a commitment to the economic, quantitative, and credit aspects of research.

Quantitative Analysis

Quantitative analysis, including estimation of holding-period returns and option-adjusted spreads (OAS) and durations, is used to evaluate individual securities and portfolio structures. We stress each potential structure to see how it performs in different interest rate and yield curve environments and to determine the risk–return characteristics inherent in the portfolio. We perform sensitivity analysis on the results by changing volatility, the shape of the curve, spreads, and prepayment levels in an attempt to achieve an "optimum" duration structure relative to our forecasts and our confidence in those forecasts.

The choice of structures for mortgage-backed securities portfolios is dramatic. Stripping activities and new CMO structures have created very-long-duration instruments, such as PO STRIPS and inverse floaters, and negative-duration instruments such as IO STRIPS. As a result, the decision on which barbell structure to use becomes complicated; the decision is not just between the 2-year and 10-year barbells but also between the minus 15-year and minus 18-year barbells. That combination has the expected barbell risk, but it also has a complicating factor: our level of confidence in the actual duration numbers of the component securities. The mortgage-backed market is not like the Treasury market, in which duration is mathematically determined; nor is it like the corporate markets, in which virtually all the dealers and investors come close to agreement on their effective duration estimates of callable corporates.

In the mortgage market, especially for STRIP securities, which are sensitive to prepayment assumptions, the dealer estimates on duration can vary widely. For example, on one IO STRIP, we have seen duration estimates ranging from minus 2 years from one dealer to minus 18 years from another. The reason for such disparities is that dealer prepayment models, which are a major influence in the duration estimate, may be affected differently by current market developments. Some dealers use only the seven-year Treasury to drive their models, and other models have important term-structure slope and shape characteristics built into them. As a result, prepayment estimates differ, and therefore, so do the durations. Without confidence in the prepayment estimate, you cannot have much confidence in the durations of the component securities or the duration structure of a portfolio. Portfolio managers must understand how the dealers' prepayments are estimated and whether they have revised their models to reflect current economic and housing conditions.

The Investment Process

An overview of the investment process for MBS is illustrated in **Figure 1**. The mortgage-specific investment process begins with the estimation of prepayment rates for a variety of MBS in light of our weekly economic forecasts. After making spot prepayment forecasts and testing their sensitivity to rate changes and time, we perform several quantitative tests to determine the attractiveness of individual securities and their potential role in a portfolio. Finally, the formal portfolio process begins: combining our risk and return estimates into the optimal portfolio.

Prepayment Forecasts

The investment process relies heavily on forecasts of prepayments, which affect cash flows and yield. Prepayments are required for OAS analysis and to calculate effective duration. Prepayments do not always move in the obvious way with changes in interest rates. For example, in 1990, an investor may have decided to construct a long-duration portfolio because of a belief, later proven to be correct, that interest rates were declining. In the MBS market, this

Figure 1. Alliance's Investment Process

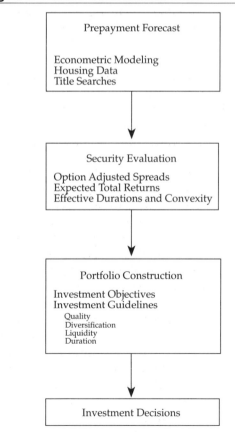

Source: Alliance Capital Management L.P.

might have led to purchases of low-coupon GNMAs and PO STRIPS, both longer duration instruments.

In fact, some of the best-performing instruments in 1990 were IOs, which are supposed to exhibit negative duration and should perform poorly as interest rates decline. The performance of IOs was superior even though interest rates declined as predicted. Estimates of duration assume a link between interest rate changes and prepayment changes, which then affect cash flows. When that link is not strong or seems to be broken, the validity of duration estimates is very low. This is what happened in 1990. Rates declined, so IOs might be expected to perform poorly, given their negative duration. Because of the recession, however, consumer confidence was low, which slowed down housing turnover, and housing prices were falling, which helped restrain refinancing (and therefore prepayments). As a result, IOs exhibited very strong performance.

The 1990 example illustrates an important point: Duration estimates are based only on rate changes, and their importance in determining price changes and performance varies over time. At times, rate changes dominate, but at other times, factors not in the duration calculation are more important.

No simple option model can be used to analyze the options embedded in mortgage securities. A closed-form model would be convenient, but the problem is far too complex. The cash flows realized in a mortgage security are a function not only of the interest rate at some point in time but also of the path of rates leading up to that time. In addition, homeowners do not always exercise their prepayment option efficiently. Many prepay their below-market-rate mortgages because they have sold their homes. Others do not refinance, even though their rates are higher than the market rate. Thus, predicting prepayments requires estimating what proportions will be efficiently, and inefficiently, exercised.

Normal housing turnover accounts for some prepayment activity, but refinancing activity can have a much larger effect over shorter periods, such as in the current market. The goal is to determine the combined strengths of the propensity to move and the propensity to refinance. We envision four teams in mortgage prepayment forecasting—the A, B, C, and D teams. The A team is the group that is *able* to refinance because of favorable incomes and home values, *anxious* to do so, and *aware* of refinancing opportunities. The B team is the group that is left after the A team leaves a mortgage pool—the *burnout* group, which does not prepay readily.

Prepayment rates tend to increase, maybe even spike, as interest rates come down, and then the prepayment levels decline again (i.e., they "burn out"). The A team self-selects itself out of the group, leaving the B team. As an example, some Ginnie Mae 15 percents are still outstanding. The B team is sometimes also referred to as the "brain-dead" group because they have not refinanced. This is a little harsh, because they may have good reasons not to refinance a high-coupon mortgage. For example, if someone expects to move soon or has a low mortgage balance, refinancing may not make sense because of taxes and attorney costs.

The C team exhibits a new phenomenon in the mortgage market—*curtailment*. Curtailment refers to early partial payment of a mortgage. The C team is that group of homeowners who disrupt the bank's amortization schedule by paying a little extra each month, a process known as curtailing the mortgage. Paying part of a mortgage off early makes it difficult to determine how old the mortgage is. In fact, the agencies have had to come back and issue new statistics on mortgage age. Once, if a mortgage was issued in Year 1, it was expected to mature in Year 30. If the mortgagor has been nibbling away at the principal, however, the loan will mature earlier, and some of its characteristics will be changed. Prepayments change as a mortgage ages, so knowing the age of a mortgage is important.

The D team prepays because of *death, divorce, disaster,* and *default*. This team's prepayments are usually independent of interest rates and normal housing turnover.

In estimating prepayment rates, we try to assess the relative weight of each team. Individual pools and aggregates still populated with A team players will be more responsive to prepayment opportunities than pools with mostly B team players.

Economic Factors

The logical sequence of how economic events affect prepayments is illustrated in **Figure 2**. The transfer effect occurs as workers move to areas experiencing economic growth; mobility creates prepayments. The income effect leads homeowners to "trade up." The correlation between personal income and housing expenditures is very strong. The third factor is an interest rate effect, which can cause prepayments to go either way. The rate effect causes homeowners to view their low-rate mortgages as a source of wealth, almost as an asset. A 4 percent mortgage in this market would be considered a valued possession and a cheap source of financing. A low-rate mortgage can restrain prepayments in that homeowners with such mortgages will be less inclined to move because they would have to pay a higher rate on a new mortgage. In contrast, homeowners with high-rate mortgages (relative to current

Figure 2. Economic Factors Used in Mortgage Market Analysis

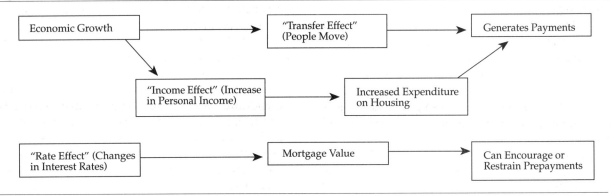

Source: Bear, Stearns & Co., Inc.

rates) are eager to refinance or look for new housing, thus creating prepayments.

Economic Data

Three major types of economic data are inputs to the MBS valuation process: interest rates, housing data, and some nonhousing statistics.

▨ *Interest rates.* An analyst must examine interest rates across the entire maturity spectrum because mortgage security prices are based on a range of maturities. For example, many adjustable rate mortgages (ARMs) are priced off the one-year Treasury rate. Five- and seven-year balloons price off the shorter intermediate Treasury rates. Fifteen and 30-year mortgages price off the 5- to 10-year Treasury rates. All of these types of mortgages may be viewed as partial substitutes for each other, inviting prepayment when one rate is lower than the other, when the certainty of fixed payments outweighs the slightly higher rate than is available on ARMS, or when fixed rates hit some threshold level such as single digits. Also, some securities' behavior is determined by maturities or durations far from their own, such as some tranches of CMOs.

In addition to the level of rates, the path of rates is important. For any given mortgage pool, if the able, anxious, and aware A team has selected itself out of the pool, and only the burned-out B team members are left (or very few A team and mostly B team members), they will be much less responsive to changes in rates.

▨ *Housing data.* A variety of housing-related data are available to help predict prepayments. These include the National Association of Realtors (NAR) housing affordability index (NAR also publishes a "first-time buyer affordability" index, which gives some indication of likely prepayment rates stemming from purchases); the National Association of Home Builders (NAHB) survey of home builders regarding potential home buyer traffic; single-family

home sales; the median price of existing homes sold; housing starts; and title searches. Another factor is the Mortgage Bankers Association (MBA) application volume indexes: How many and what type of applications are mortgage bankers taking for new mortgages? What proportion is for home purchases, and what proportion for refinancing?

We also look at the figures released every month by the Government National Mortgage Association (Ginnie Mae), the Federal National Mortgage Association (Fannie Mae), and the Federal Home Loan Bank Board (Freddie Mac) showing the prepayment histories on the securities in which we are interested.

As an example of useful data, **Figure 3** shows model home traffic as reported by NAHB since 1989. This statistic is an indicator of the general state of the economy and a leading indicator of home sales and housing turnover—and therefore, of prepayments. Judging from recent trends, the new housing market does not appear to be very robust. The 30 percent of home builders reporting high traffic is still lower than those reporting low traffic, but it is a dramatic

Figure 3. Model Home Traffic

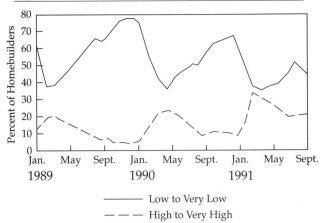

Source: Alliance Capital Management L.P., based on data from National Association of Home Builders.

improvement over the recent figure of 10 percent reporting high traffic.

Sales activity has been extremely low in the past several years, as indicated in **Figure 4**. These NAHB data are for the volume of actual sales, measured in qualitative terms such as "poor" and "good to excellent." The growth in traffic must be followed by a growth in sales before concluding that housing is coming back and prepayments from turnover will rise.

Mortgage application volume is an indicator of potential prepayment activity. **Figure 5** presents weekly data collected by MBA on the number of mortgage applications its members received. The chart shows the volume of applications on an index basis, broken down into refinancing and purchase. A spike in applications occurred in late 1991 and peaked in January 1992, reflecting the low point in interest rates to that date. The end of the spike probably reflects some "burnout" and the subsequent climb in rates. Mortgage application volume was divided about 50/50 between refinancing and new home purchases despite the disparity in these indexes. The MBA also provides application information by type of mortgage instrument—adjustable or fixed rate—which provides some idea of the originating sector for the new supply of mortgages soon to enter the market. Such data can help in analyzing technical marketplace factors such as supply and demand trends.

As a final reality check on our forecasts, we review title search data provided by Advanced Factor Services. It tallies title searches performed by the largest title companies in the United States and links them to the underlying loans and any MBS that include those loans. Because a title search is performed when a new mortgage is about to be made on a property (either because the owner is moving or is refinancing), title search data are useful in predicting near-term prepayments.

▓ *Other macroeconomic statistics.* We also review some nonhousing statistics, including personal income and consumer confidence data. Because the correlation between personal income and housing expenditures is so strong, rising personal income is likely to be accompanied by an increase in trading-up activity. Consumer confidence also is important when potential homeowners contemplate the largest single purchase they are likely to make. Low confidence levels are associated with low housing sales.

Investment Selection

For purposes of investment, the mortgage market can be divided into sectors in several ways. These include Ginnie Mae as opposed to conventional loans; premium as opposed to discount securities; IO as opposed to PO instruments; collateral as opposed to planned amortization classes; or by type of payment—adjustable rate, fixed rate, or balloon.

Technical factors can be important in sector selection. What is the Resolution Trust Corporation doing? How does the positive yield curve affect CMO production? What is the impact of capital regulation on banks, thrifts, and insurance companies? Low corporate capital demand creates demand for mortgage securities because the corporations are not issuing securities. Difficulties in commercial real estate may lead investors into the residential mortgage market. Guidelines set forth in the Financial Institutions Reform, Recovery, and Enforcement Act and the Basle agreements affect what banks and other financial institutions may do in the market.

Individual security selection in the mortgage market is made more difficult because each security

Figure 4. Builders' Sales Activity

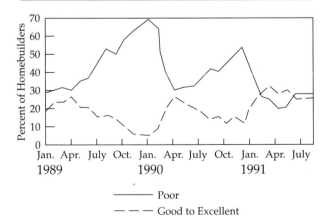

Source: Alliance Capital Management L.P., based on data from National Association of Home Builders.

Figure 5. Index of Mortgage Application Volume

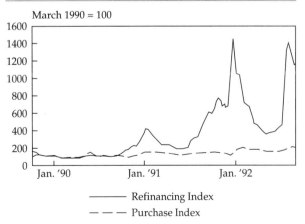

Source: Alliance Capital Management L.P., based on data from Mortgage Bankers Association.

is unique. Each instrument has its own weighted-average coupon and weighted-average maturity, which can affect prepayment behavior. Combined with geographic and other idiosyncratic features, each security presents a slightly different history and outlook.

Economic statistics become important during the security selection process. Until recently, when looking for IOs or high-premium securities having prepayment-sensitive performance, we preferred those originated in the Northeast. The factors hurting housing values in the Northeast resulted in lower prepayments and made those securities more attractive to hold in a portfolio. The decline in employment and housing values slowed prepayment speeds, resulting in longer amortization of the premium prices and higher returns. Typically, high-premium securities from California have been less desirable to hold because their prepayment rates are usually much more rapid. Recently, the Northeast has shown some housing strength, and other areas are showing weakness. This offers swap opportunities and demonstrates the need for timely data.

Conclusion

Many individual characteristics of the mortgage-related and other fixed-income securities must be examined. We address as many as possible with publicly available economic statistics from a variety of sources. The key is to acquire the information on a timely basis direct from the provider and not wait for commentary from a secondary source, such as a broker–dealer. Then, act on the information quickly, incorporating the implications into forecasts and quantitative analyses as fast as possible.

A wide range of economic factors and uncertainties affect the valuation of mortgage securities. As in any specialized field, we have developed our own jargon, tailored analyses, and a wide range of "nonmainstream" economic data that we use daily. Without fast response, these data lose their effectiveness, but without the data, we would not be able to make informed investment decisions.

Question and Answer Session

Chris P. Dialynas
Robert W. Kopprasch, CFA

Question: How do you factor the high cost of hedging European bonds—that is, having to go back and forth between foreign currency and dollars—into your analysis of the role of international bonds in a U.S. bond portfolio?

Dialynas: We factor the cost indirectly. The cost of hedging can be and has been quite high recently. For example, a German bond yielding 8 percent might cost 3 percent to hedge on an annual basis. We incorporate that yield reduction into our analysis, compare our expectations of interest rates abroad, compare the price appreciation of that change with the yield, and transform the results into a total return framework just as we would for domestic bonds.

Question: Please comment on how your portfolios differ from their benchmarks.

Kopprasch: We try not to make a duration bet so interest rate changes do not overwhelm what we consider our value bets in the portfolio. Our portfolio does vary from the index in structure. If we choose to hold IOs that came from, for example, Fannie Mae 9s, the Fannie Mae 9s are in the index in their entirety, but our portfolio only has the interest STRIP. As a result, we are short something that is in the index— the principal. We have a duration that matches or comes close to the index but has a very different distribution across duration buckets. The index usually does not contain anything that has a negative duration, so if we

choose to hold a negative duration instrument, we must also hold some relatively higher duration instruments to achieve a portfolio duration close to the index duration.

Dialynas: Our duration guidelines would generally allow us to hold portfolio durations ranging from 75 percent to 1.25 percent of the prescribed portfolio bogey. We are willing to deviate from index sector distribution by a considerable margin, perhaps as much as 25 or 30 percent, depending on the degree of conviction we have in the inputs we are using to evaluate that sector.

Question: Option-adjusted models are now generic products. Are there good ones and bad ones, or do they all do the same job?

Dialynas: We tend to develop our models internally, and we compare them to other standard models. The outcomes are not very different. From a generic output viewpoint, most models seem to use the same technology and produce approximately the same results. The benefit we derive from using our own model is that it is more flexible. We can enter the kinds of volatility distributions, interest rates, or yield curve shape changes we want into our model and get an answer that might be different from that of a conventional model.

Question: Would your option-adjusted model be useful in equity valuation—equity being the ultimate option?

Dialynas: The problem is difficult, because the equity is the option on everything else. Changes in volatility and the performance of specific classes or sectors of the equity market are probably strongly linked, although I have not tested this relationship.

Question: Investment objectives are an important element in the portfolio construction aspect of your work. Please define your investment objective categories and explain their risk–return profiles.

Kopprasch: A typical investment objective on an institutional portfolio is total return. Most institutions concentrate on total return and do not worry about accounting income as managers of mutual fund portfolios are forced to do. A mutual fund usually has an income constraint, which may cause the fund to buy certain securities that would not be bought for a total return portfolio. Probably most institutional clients will accept something like the Salomon Brothers Mortgage Index or the Lehman Mortgage Index as their benchmark. Because we are measured against a benchmark, we try to structure our portfolio so it will outperform a particular benchmark. Yet the overall risk characteristics are similar to the benchmark duration.

Question: Are there simple rules for maximum yield and minimum risk in bond portfolios? Can some portfolios statistically dominate others for extended periods of time in the bond market?

Dialynas: No simple rules exist,

and no static portfolio would be the portfolio for all seasons. The easy way to understand that answer is by examining the changes in the shape of the yield curve. In a three-year period, it has gone from negative to positive to flattening again. Mortgages have substantially different returns as yield curve shapes change.

Question: How will the new adjustable rate mortgage (ARM) funds change the market? What are their risks?

Kopprasch: These funds have provided a dramatic new demand for ARMs just as the thrifts are exiting that market. Thrifts used to absorb all new production. The ARM funds have come along as interest rates have come way down. A security that prices at 275 basis points over the one-year Treasury (assuming its price is not too high) has a real yield advantage. Many people are moving from money markets to these funds. Shearson sold a fund that totaled $42 million in April and hit $500 million by December. A tremendous amount of money is going into all ARM funds.

At the same time, ARM prices have now gone up to historic levels. New ARM funds have really increased the demand for ARMs. Initially, we worked with someone who advised never buying an ARM over par. We had to ignore this advice because no ARMs were priced under par. The advice then changed: Do not buy any ARMs over 101 (later 105), but we are not buying any ARMs at 105. ARM prices are as high as they are for several reasons, but largely it is the demand, which we have never seen before.

The risk in the ARM portfolio depends on the structure. First, if it is a straight ARM portfolio, the portfolio yield will lag interest rate changes. Consider a pool of one-year Treasury ARMs. Typically, the pool will not have all the loans repricing on one date—for example, 10 percent might reprice in January, 4 percent in February, and so on. As rates move up, a small portion is repricing every month back to the current rate, but the rest of it is not. This lag in the rate was very beneficial as rates were coming down. The ARMs were paying "too high" a coupon, which is one reason the price was going up.

Second, many ARM funds have a small slice of IOs in them. ARMs usually have a duration longer than a year because of life and periodic caps, and many ARM funds were using IOs to provide negative duration to reduce the overall portfolio duration.

Third, most ARM funds are leveraged so they can increase yield. They take some existing securities, pledge them to borrow more money, and then take that money and buy more ARMs. In general, the risk involved is fairly low. With a short-duration portfolio, the borrowing, which is typically weekly, does not produce a gross duration mismatch. They are not buying long bonds with short funding, but they are buying something with a duration longer than a year. They do this because they can fund the ARMs at 4 percent, or somewhere in that range, and get a 6 percent yield, so they are adding that excess yield to the portfolio.

Obviously, leverage works both ways. As the yield curve starts to flatten and ARM prices fall, the portfolio could decline 140 percent because it contains more ARMs than equity. This is not a major risk, but ARM funds are not money market funds, and they can and do fluctuate in value.

Selecting Equity Securities

Elaine Garzarelli
Director of Quantitative Strategies
Lehman Brothers

> Four factors can be used to read the stock market, with each accounting for roughly a quarter of what makes the market move: economic factors, Federal Reserve policy, valuation, and investor sentiment.

The set of indicators I use to read the stock market are based on the four basic factors that move the market: the economy, Federal Reserve policy, valuation, and sentiment. Each factor accounts for about 25 percent of what makes the market move.

Market Movers

My indicators provide buy and sell signals totally against what most people believe, because that is the way the indicators are designed. A buy signal is anything above 65 percent after I have had a sell signal. A sell signal is 30 percent or lower on the indicators. When I get a sell, we go to cash and stay in cash until the indicator is 65 percent. Then we get 100 percent invested and stay that way until the indicators go back to 30 percent.

Take sentiment, for example. When too many investment advisors are bullish, the indicator for sentiment turns negative. In early 1992, as calculated by *Investor's Intelligence*, 75 percent of investment advisors were bullish on the stock market. Today, that percentage has dropped to about 65 percent. When it goes below 59 percent, I will upgrade my indicator.

I have applied this econometric model to four additional stock markets—Japan, Germany, France, and the United Kingdom. If the data are available, the model can be applied to other markets. The data, however, are not available in all countries. For example, earnings in France come out only once a year. Thus, earnings cannot be used with any great degree of reliability because they must be interpolated during the year. Furthermore, few countries have sentiment indicators. About 65 percent of the indicators are transferrable, however, so the model has worked fairly well for at least some non-U.S. markets.

Economic Factors

Twenty-five percent of what moves the market is the economy, but not the economy alone. The first derivative is what moves the market—the changes in earnings, industrial production, real gross domestic product (GDP), and the other economic variables. The changes are what the market considers important, and it will keep going up until it sees the economy's growth rate peaking and then beginning to slow.

A growing economy is not always good for the stock market. The early stages of the growth are good, but when it begins to slow, the stock market peaks and then falls. One of the best indicators is to take the year-to-year change in industrial production and try to predict when it will peak. Absolute levels are more difficult to predict than the percent change in the economic factor. Based on my econometric models, industrial production will not peak, on a year-to-year change basis, until the third quarter of 1993. This provides more than a year before the economy's momentum will peak and thereafter exert a negative influence on stock prices.

When the market crashed in the fourth quarter of 1987, earnings were reaching their peak on the S&P 500, on a year-to-year change basis. Earnings were 40 percent higher than the previous year's fourth-quarter level. Real GDP also reached its peak in the fourth quarter. Everybody was bullish.

The valuation part of my indicators was bearish for more than a year before the crash, but valuation is only 25 percent of what moves the market. The economy was not ready. The negative ingredients in the economy were not sufficiently strong to give me a sell signal until September 1, 1987. On that date, the Federal Reserve raised the discount rate, another market mover. The crash took place on October 19, so we had time to get out of the market.

To analyze the economy, you must know peaks and troughs. We are far away from the peak, but we are coming out of this recession. Housing is up. Consumer sentiment is up. Interest rates will probably trade within a 50-basis-point range in either direction for the next year and therefore should not be a problem. In the long term, I am bullish on interest rates and inflation. This recovery may be weaker than normal because we have much debt to unwind, which will drag down the economy. Profits in 1992 will be up only about 20 percent compared with the normal 35 percent gain coming out of a recession. In 1993, the gain in profits should be another 11 percent. The recovery is weaker than usual, but it is fairly good. Twenty-five percent of my indicators are currently bullish.

Federal Reserve Policy

Federal Reserve policy influences all the other variables indirectly. When the Fed tightens its monetary policy, the market is bearish, and when it loosens up, the market is bullish.

We have just gone through a downward correction in the stock market. The Dow dropped 3 percent; the S&P 500, 4.5 percent; and the NASDAQ industrials, 8 percent—a substantial correction. Every time at this stage of the cycle, however, a correction of between 10 and 15 percent in the stock market is preceded by a rise of 20 or 25 percent in the three-month Treasury bill rate. The Treasury bill rate bottomed on February 15, 1992, at 3.72 percent. That multiplied by 1.20 is the critical level in the Treasury bill rate that would precede a decline in the stock market. Currently, the Treasury bill rate is about 4 percent. Reaching 4.5 or 4.6 percent, which is the average rate, would require the Fed to tighten interest rates, which probably will not happen until after the presidential election. Thus, this set of indicators will look good for a while.

The money supply is growing. If the economy stalls, as it did last year, the Fed would be much more willing to ease rates to make sure the economy continues to move up. Last year when the Fed thought everything was going well, it stopped easing, and everything went back down again.

When did this recession actually bottom? The National Bureau of Economic Research indicates it was in April 1991, when we hit a low in industrial production. Industrial production started up in 1991 and then came back down in 1992, but it did not go lower than it had been. Industrial production did not hit its low when profits did, about December 1991 or January 1992, which—from a stock market perspective—is when the recession ended. When history is written, however, the bottom may appear to have been in April 1991. According to stock-market-related indicators, the double-dip can be classified as the real trough. This means the bull market will continue a little longer.

Valuation

I use both a bottom-up and a top-down approach for determining S&P 500 earnings. My bottom-up process uses 60 econometric models for S&P industry groups, including the steel, automobile, home appliance, retailing, and banking industries. Each model has 14 equations and includes economic inputs for the factors that are important for the industry. I run the models once a month to estimate earnings for each industry, and then I add these estimates to get the S&P earnings.

My top-down model is a least-squares model that looks at aggregate price–cost ratios for the nonfarm economy. The inputs include GDP projections through the end of the coming year, the capitalization rate, earnings from the rest of the world, the dollar exchange rate, and profits in the national income accounts. The model has about an 88 percent coefficient of determination on a year-to-year change basis.

My bottom-up and top-down numbers rarely match, so I spend two weeks every month going through every industry and adjusting the numbers until the bottom-up result is within about 0.5 percent of the top-down result. This is a good methodology; it requires a lot of structure and you must keep your emotions out, which is why it works.

Earnings alone are not enough to predict stock prices. You need an equation to predict the price–earnings ratio (P/E). The P/E for the S&P 500 is a function of three figures: the three-month Treasury bill rate, the 30-year Treasury bond yield, and the rate of inflation. Based on data going back to 1954, the regression analysis has an r^2 of about 85 percent. I never predict interest rates; I just use what is available today. The Treasury bill rate is at 4 percent, the Treasury bond yield is at 8 percent, the rate of inflation is at 3 percent, so the fair P/E for the market today should be 15.8 times earnings. My earnings number for 1992 is 27 and 30 for 1993. With the S&P 500 at the 406 or 407 level, it is at 13.5 times earnings, and it should be at 15.8. The fair value for the S&P 500 on 1993 earnings is about 471, which is about 3,670 on the Dow.

In a recession, valuing the market on trailing earnings is dangerous because earnings fall and the P/E is high. Also, in this particular cycle, write-offs in 1991 on the S&P 500 were 27 percent of earnings; that is, earnings would have been 27 percent higher without all the write-offs that were taken.

Some analysts look at earnings as reported in the newspaper, and others adjust earnings to reflect the write-offs. To determine whether this difference affects the market, we counted how many of the S&P 500 companies reported earnings write-offs in their quarterly statements during the past 30 years. We found that earnings as reported in the newspaper were correlated 63 percent with the stock market and earnings adjusted for write-offs were correlated 92 percent.

Many people examine trailing earnings instead of future earnings and conclude that the market is overvalued. We were in a recession, and the earnings had write-offs of 27 percent. Consequently, the P/E appears to be 40 times earnings, the highest in history. If the market considered this, the Dow would be at 2,000 today, not 3,200, which is further proof that trailing earnings is not the way to value the market.

The market does not always stop at fair value. On the way up, the market often goes above fair value. Before the crash of 1987, the market was overvalued by 1,000 points. It goes above fair value if monetary policy is loose and profits are far from peaking. To determine how much the market can go above fair value, look at such relationships as the ratios of the S&P earnings yield and the S&P cash flow yield to the level of long- and short-term rates. When these ratios reach certain extremes, the market will peak or bottom. The market-peak point is currently above 4,000 on the Dow, and interest rates may not rise for a long time. If so, the market could exceed fair value.

Investor Sentiment

The fourth factor that moves the market is sentiment. Too many investors are bullish these days. Cash levels of mutual funds and switch funds today are 4.3 percent, the lowest in history. Before the 1987 crash, cash levels of mutual and switch funds were 4.7 percent. In fact, before most bull market peaks, cash levels have been between 4.0 and 4.5 percent.

The low cash level does not necessarily mean a market peak is imminent. A few times when cash levels fell, the market continued to rise for more than a year. That was also a period when initial public offerings (IPOs) were rampant, however. Increased speculation does not necessarily mean the market must stop in its tracks. It will stop when the Fed tightens up on interest rates.

The current period most resembles early 1972 in the market's valuation, the number of IPOs, and the cash level. From 1972 until January 1973, a nice bull market prevailed. It went up and did not stop until the Fed tightened its monetary policy. I predict an-

other 6 to 12 months of bull market and stock market gains that will strongly outperform bonds and cash.

The Market Outlook

The market outlook is good. We are rather bullish in an environment in which you would think we should not be. My indicators for industry are currently at 78 percent, and they must fall to 30 percent or lower to be a major sell signal. This probably will not happen until the second quarter of 1993. If the Treasury bill rate goes up to 4.5 or 4.6 percent, and a major sell takes place, the market could decline between 20 and 50 percent. Before that, an intermediate-term bull market correction of 10 or 12 percent could occur. Without a major sell or a Treasury bill rate increase, all corrections should be limited to between 4 and 7 percent.

The best industries to be in during the recovery period are the cyclicals—automobiles, appliances, general merchandise chains, regional banks, semiconductors, computers, paper, and chemicals. The worst groups to be in are drugs, health care, telephones, electric utilities, natural gas, and foods. With S&P earnings growing dramatically, we are emerging from a depressed economy. The key to outperforming is to select industries and stocks with earnings growth better than the growth in the S&P 500. Only cyclical groups will allow managers to beat the 22 percent growth. In mid-1993, when the S&P earnings slow again, I will switch back into foods, drugs, and more-defensive industries.

The 1987 market crash could have caused the economy to fall dramatically if confidence had been lost. The day of the crash, Alan Greenspan, Chairman of the Board of Governors of the Federal Reserve, eased interest rates until the market stopped falling and confidence was restored. This crash in the stock market had no effect on the economy. The high level of debt today, as a share of GDP, can only be compared to 1929. The system could actually collapse if Greenspan should allow the banks to fail and tighten credit, thus preventing the recovery from taking hold. Real problems could result. He watches everything closely, however, and holds the hand of the economy as if it were a 2-year-old child. If you do that long enough, the child will eventually grow up and be able to take care of himself. This did not work in 1929 because the Fed made major mistakes: It allowed banks to fail and the money supply to fall by 50 percent. That will not happen today.

The level of unemployment will be higher in the future, especially among banks, insurance companies, and attorneys—a white-collar recession. As a result, inflation will be lower, which will reduce bond yields. Lower bond yields mean higher P/E ratios and a good stock market.

During the next four to six years, only bonds and stocks will offer double-digit returns. Cash will continue at 4 percent. Real estate will not do too much. Gold, oriental rugs, or jewelry will not be good investments. The period ahead will be one of much unwinding, but it will be bullish because of higher unemployment and lower inflation. As an economist, the most important factor I examine for any foreign country is its rate of inflation, not its GDP, because inflation is the key to a healthy economy.

Question and Answer Session

Elaine Garzarelli

Question: Is the rate of change in the rate of change a good indicator?

Garzarelli: The rate of change in the rate of change also works as an indicator, but the market does not look at it. It leads the cycle so much that it can provide a false reading.

Question: Accrual accounting on assets is an act of faith. We record as revenue money not yet received, and we deduct from expenses money spent on assets that are supposed to produce revenue in the future. As a result, P/Es are actually understated because the earnings are overstated. How do you deal with what normal P/Es should be, particularly with regard to write-offs?

Garzarelli: Recently, I empirically tested whether I should use some write-offs in my models. The evidence is clear that earnings net of write-offs are more highly correlated with the market than are reported earnings. My model assumes that once a company has taken a write-off, it will not be taking more in the future. Write-offs cause pauses in the market because the market has to figure out what they mean.

Question: Given that your bottom-up forecast differs from your macro forecast, how often does the bottom-up forecast lead you to change your macro forecast?

Garzarelli: When emerging from a recession, the bottom-up approach usually gives me a higher forecast than the top-down approach. Often, Wall Street strategists underestimate

the first year of earnings. This time, I increased my top-down (macro) estimate by half of the difference between it and the bottom-up. The bottom-up forecast does not lead me to change my estimate of how strong the economy will be, because the macro forecasts are inputs into each industry. I add all the industry earnings to get the total. For the top-down model, the standard error could be 3 or 4 percent.

Question: If the model is so good, why is forecasting imperfect?

Garzarelli: I sometimes make mistakes because I do not follow my indicators. In 1987, the first time I ever ran a mutual fund, I got out before the crash. In February 1988, however, when I got a buy signal, I wrote a buy report and got all my clients in, but I did not get my fund invested because I was too cautious. This ruined my performance.

Other times, the forecast is invalidated by outside events such as the invasion of Kuwait. I thought we would have a bull market for another six months, and then the war happened. It totally changed my models. The invasion of Kuwait caused oil prices to double. As a result, the economy slipped into an unexpected recession. We thought it would be a soft landing. I got a sell signal a week later, which I did not expect. I do not know if that was a mistake or just a quick turnaround. Typically, an event would have to change the economic structure to change my indicators. Most mistakes are based on emotion rather than analysis.

Question: How would you compare individual and institutional investors in the current market?

Garzarelli: The individual investor is coming into the market for the first time in 20 years because the rate of return on certificates of deposit (CDs) is so small. More of that is likely to happen. The turnout is much larger when I talk about retail rather than institutional investing, which was not the case when the rate on CDs was 11 or 12 percent. A whole new educational process is taking place. Individual investors are not used to the stock market. They want to start with utilities because they can get a nice rate of return in dividends, but they are becoming sophisticated. If cash levels range between 3.5 and 4.5 percent during the next few years, more individual investors will enter the market.

Question: Suppose the economy is stronger than we expect, or the Dow weaker, and short-term interest rates begin to move up toward 5 or 6 percent again. How hot do you think that money is?

Garzarelli: A rise in short rates could take money away from the market, and a market correction of 10 or 15 percent would occur if that happened. Then the market would be so cheap relative to cash that it would probably go back up again. My biggest fear is that the economy will recover too fast. That would make industrial production peak earlier than expected, which would curtail the bull market. I like a steady recovery, which I think we are experiencing.

Using International Economic Inputs

Jeffrey J. Diermeier, CFA
Managing Partner
Brinson Partners, Inc.

Comparative valuation—one of four techniques generally used to position assets strategically in a global portfolio—involves estimating a level of intrinsic value across securities or asset classes, comparing those values to observed prices, taking risk into consideration, and building portfolios based on risk-adjusted value.

The use of international economic inputs in the global portfolio decision process is analogous to using domestic economic inputs in the domestic portfolio decision process. The additional challenge of dealing with multiple currencies adds a layer of complexity that must be dealt with successfully before a truly potential global portfolio can be constructed. Structuring the risky asset decision also is more complex for global portfolios.

An additional challenge, not discussed in this presentation, is decision hierarchy: Should we first decide what securities or industries to buy and then let the country decisions fall out or make the country decisions first and then make industry and individual security selections within the countries?

Comparative Valuation

The decision on how to position assets strategically generally involves one or more of four types of techniques: comparative valuation, business cycle anticipation, liquidity/flow of funds, and technical analysis. Some people make asset allocation and investment decisions based on business cycle anticipation or leading indicators. For global analysis, the Center for International Business Cycle Research at Columbia University provides a wealth of objective leading indicator data. Other investors focus on liquidity or flow of funds, taking a look at monetary policy and trying to capture, for example, the essence of what happens to financial assets in a monetarily overstimulated economy. Some people use technical analysis structures to reach their asset allocation decisions.

The focus of this presentation is on comparative valuation, which involves estimating a level of intrinsic value across securities or asset classes, comparing these values to observed prices, taking risk into consideration, and building portfolios based on risk-adjusted value. Our firm uses a standardized three-stage valuation model in which the estimated value of an asset (V_E) equals the sum of the discounted value in a growth-to-normal stage (V_{S1}), a normal growth stage (V_N), and a mature stage (V_M). If we were operating solely within the U.S. equity market, using the S&P 500 as a proxy for the market, we would use a two-stage model because the U.S. market is mature enough to skip the middle stage. In many countries, however, the second stage is relevant, particularly in a growth country like Hong Kong.

The key functional inputs to the three-stage valuation framework are the estimates of cash flow to be paid to the investor in the growth to normal period, the growth of cash flow in the normal period, the transition period pattern of growth by which normal growth approaches mature growth, the rate of cash flow growth in the mature period, and the appropriate discount rates that convert each estimate of cash flow to a present value. From a strict valuation standpoint, economic inputs are relevant only if they bring information to bear on the estimates of the cash flows themselves or on the elements that go into estimating the appropriate discount rate(s).

At the aggregate level both in the United States and on a global scale, economists do provide information for investors to incorporate into their decision making. At the broadest level, the growth of aggregate economic activity is closely related to the growth of capital markets, but few attempts have been made to link growth in economic output to security returns over long periods of time.

Figure 1 compares the U.S. investable capital market capitalization, which currently totals about $13 trillion dollars, with U.S. gross domestic product (GDP). Incorporated into the U.S. investable capital market is the market value of all common stocks, fixed-income securities, cash equivalents, real estate, and venture capital. This aggregation avoids double counting where possible. For example, the portion of real estate that has been securitized is not included in the real estate segment. The investable capital market is a measure of the value of the capital market in which we can invest.

The growth of GDP (7.4 percent) and the growth in the total value of the capital market (7.2 percent) are closely related over long periods of time, as this figure demonstrates. During the 1949–91 period, inflation ran about 4.5 percent a year, so real growth in the investable capital market and GDP was about 3 percent.

Figure 2 compares global investable capital market capitalization and industrial country GDP. The data are for the roughly 20 industrial countries included in the Morgan Stanley Capital International Index. Global investable capital market capitalization equals the U.S. investable capital market plus estimates of the size of the non-U.S. equity and fixed-income markets. In dollar terms, the GDP of the 20 industrial countries grew at a compound annual rate of about 9.8 percent and the size of the global investable capital market grew 9 percent. The growth rate of GDP in U.S. dollars for the Organization for Economic Cooperation and Development (OECD) countries during that same period was 9.4 percent. Over-

all, inflation during the period was between 5.0 and 5.5 percent, so the real growth rate for those countries was about 4 percent. The growth of the aggregate economy defines, as a national income identity, the growth of national income.

Figures 1 and 2 do not show the return to capital markets but rather the growth in their aggregate size. **Figure 3** presents a framework for taking an aggregate capital market growth rate forecast and converting it to a longer term forecast of capital market returns.

Aggregate economic output growth determines the growth in income available for all factors of production: labor, capital, and transfer payments. The capital markets determine how much goes to rent, interest, and dividends. Moving from growth in the size of the aggregate capital market to an estimate of return requires making a simple adjustment. The return to the overall capital market equals the gross market yield of the capital market in the forms of dividends, interest, and rents minus net new issues as a percentage of market capitalization plus the growth in aggregate output (that is, $r = [d - n]/w + G$). This approach assumes capital market participants lay claim to a constant share of aggregate output and no change in expectations occurs that might cause price–value ratios to change.

The yield term differs from that typically used. Capital market returns are modeled in simple terms as a function of yield and growth in earnings per share, not as a function of net yield plus growth in aggregate output. Share issuance is typically captured in the growth rate by putting growth on a

Figure 1. Wealth Indexes, U.S. Investable Capital Market Capitalization and U.S. Gross Domestic Product, 1949–91

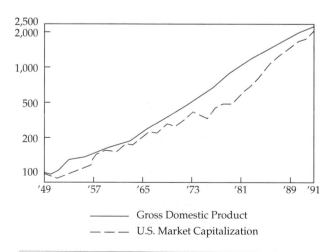

———— Gross Domestic Product

— — — U.S. Market Capitalization

Source: Brinson Partners, Inc.

Note: December 31, 1948 = 100. Preliminary data through 1991.

Figure 2. Wealth Indexes, Global Investable Capital Market Capitalization and Industrial Country Gross Domestic Product, 1960–91

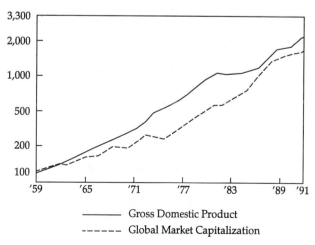

———— Gross Domestic Product

------ Global Market Capitalization

Source: Brinson Partners, Inc.

Note: December 31, 1959 = 100. Preliminary data through 1991.

Figure 3. The Capital Market Forecasting Hierarchy

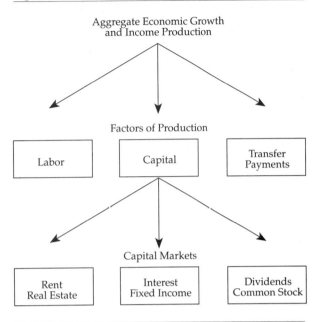

Source: Brinson Partners, Inc.

per-share basis. The understanding of net yield, which is required in this format, requires greater knowledge of the total financial structure of the market. Analysts must understand the implicit leverage of the market, how capital is raised, and propensities to pay out rather than retain cash flow. In some countries where yield rates are low, new capital is generated through additions to retained earnings rather than through robust new-equity issue markets. The new format is useful because it separates the yield concept into gross market yield and net new issues.

The assumption that capital market participants lay claim to a constant share of aggregate output may not hold. Globally, shareholders have been losing share since 1960. For example, in the OECD countries from 1960 to 1989, the GDP growth rate was 9.4 percent. The growth rate of operating surplus, which is the amount of corporate revenues left after indirect taxes, depreciation, and compensation of employees, was only 8.8 percent. The primary reason for this decline in the United States has been added compensation in the form of nonwage benefits and social security and unemployment compensation taxes.

During the 1969–89 period, Japanese shareholders have been among those losing the most in share. The GDP growth rate in Japan was 11.6 percent, but operating surplus—money available to corporations to pay interest and as profits—grew only 9.4 percent a year. This difference amounts to a 180-basis-point spread between the growth in the economy and what

was available to investors as a whole.

The fundamental investment principles of yield and growth make economic sense and are useful in research underlying forecasts of long-term returns. As a result, rather than relying on short-term economic information, focusing more on the sources of long-term economic growth proves to be more useful. **Exhibit 1** lists those sources: labor effort, capital effort, and other contributing factors. In practice, traditional purveyors of economic research devote surprisingly little time to these structural elements of production. Ultimately, labor effort is defined by the population, its willingness to work, and the training and education that it brings to bear. That work force is endowed with capital, which extends its usefulness through technological development and rational utilization. Important factors contributing to the willingness and ability of the work force and the quality of the capital stock involve the economic environment, which can foster long-term investment, the global competitive environment, and specific incentives generated by government policy. From a secular standpoint, the focus is on these variables when determining the growth and prosperity of any country.

Exhibit 1. Sources of Long-Term Economic Growth Expectations

Labor Effort	*Contributing Factors*
Population	Inflation
Labor participation rate	Level
Labor force	Stability
Percentage employed	Economic mix
Work force	Manufacturing
Hours worked per	Service
employee	Peace expectations
Total hours worked	Energy availability
Business training	Economic stability
Education	Foreign competition
	Trade relations
Capital Effort	Incentives
Capital stock (net)	Regulation
Capital employed	Tax mix
Technology/R&D	Government share of
Capacity utilization	output

Source: Brinson Partners, Inc.

The Discount Rate

The basic approach for calculating intrinsic value involves discounting expected cash flows. The discount rate (K) is calculated as follows:

$$K = [(1 + I_A)(1 + R_A)(1 + RP_{AS})] - 1,$$

where

I_A = inflation premium for country A,
R_A = real risk-free interest rate for country A, and
RP_{AS} = risk premium for security S in country A.

The discount rate is typically viewed as a function of inflation, the real risk-free interest rate, and risk premiums. Many experts say real risk-free interest rates around the world are going to converge over time. In addition, we have seen much convergence in inflation rates during the past 10 or 15 years. Furthermore, if Europe adopts a single currency, as spelled out in the Maastricht treaty, the signatory countries' inflation rates should show little divergence.

In a global framework, risk premium estimation is complicated. Bernstein and McNees discuss the risk premium as a function of risk.[1] Volatility can be a measure of risk, although an imperfect one. If risk is the basis for the risk premium, where does risk originate? Risk must come from variation in those fundamental investment principles discussed earlier. In other words, risk must arise because we cannot perfectly forecast such variables as cash flows or the discount rate. The risk premium for any security S in country A (RP_{AS}) is

$$RP_{AS} = f(IR_A, RR_A, SR_A, PCFR_S, COV_{S,O}),$$

where

IR_A = inflation risk in country A,
RR_A = real rate of risk in country A,
SR_A = sovereign risk in country A,
$PCFR_S$ = private cash flow risk for security S, and
$COV_{S,O}$ = covariance effect of security S with other securities.

The first source of the risk premium for a given security in country A is the inflation risk in that country. The second functional term in the risk premium is the real interest rate risk in country A stemming from the fact that we do not know precisely what real interest rates will be in the future. The third element of the risk premium is sovereign risk, which is the possibility that debts, such as bonds, might not get paid off because of war, a debt holiday, or other countrywide problem. Sovereign risk can be separated from the fourth term, private cash flow risk, which is the volatility of the cash flows paid to the investor brought about by variation in the fortunes of private companies. The covariance structure between the various securities will, by definition, play

[1]See Mr. Bernstein's and Mr. McNees's presentations, pp. 24-28 and 15-22, respectively.

a role in the determination of relevant risk and becomes much more complicated when moving from a single-country to a multicountry level.

Building a Portfolio

Building a global portfolio entails some unique challenges: currency allocation decisions, risky asset allocation, and the decision hierarchy—country selection as opposed to security selection. How can an investor ensure that market and currency strategies work together to maximize the performance of the entire portfolio? Currency management is more appropriately viewed as global cash management. Because the risk-free rate is embedded in every risky asset, active management of risky assets is more appropriately viewed as local currency risk-premium management. **Exhibit 2** invokes the separation theory that has been used in many capital asset pricing model analyses and puts it into a framework in which the risk-free rate is separated from the risky asset rate and the use of cash equivalents is viewed as the basis for making the currency decision.

The conventional approach is to view the portfolio decision-making process when going global as making a market decision based on local market returns and a currency decision using an exchange rate change. The combination of exchange rate changes with the local market expectation is built into a set of expected returns, and the portfolio is built on that basis.

A better framework for global currency management is to make a market decision based on a forecasted local market risk premium and a currency decision based on a cash dollar return. The cash dollar return is calculated by examining local cash returns and forecasting the exchange rate change.

There are two basic approaches to currency forecasting: the asset market approach, of which purchasing power parity theories (PPP) are a subset, and a balance of payments, or flow of funds, approach. Currencies in this framework are set so that markets clear. If market participants in country A wish to own assets in country B, they are assumed to bid up the price of country B's currency.

Our firm's focus emphasizes the PPP notion, as shown in **Figure 4**. In this case, the dollar is attractive relative to the yen. This particular forecast flows into the forecasted exchange rate change previously discussed. **Table 1** shows the components of the currency decision. For Japan, we estimate over a relevant time frame an expected local currency cash return of 5.37 percent. We think the yen is high relative to the dollar, so in dollar terms, the expected exchange rate return during that period for a yen-

Exhibit 2. Global Currency Management Framework: Separation Theory

Market Decision	Currency Decision

Conventional approach
Dollar return = local market return + Exchange rate change

Correct framework
Dollar return

$$= \left(\begin{array}{ccc} local \\ market & - & cash \\ return & & return \end{array}\right) + \left(\begin{array}{ccc} local \\ cash & + & rate \\ return & & change \end{array}\right)$$

Local market risk premium	+	Cash dollar return

Source: Brinson Partners, Inc.

based asset would be –1.23 percent. The expected cash return in dollars for the asset class of Japanese cash is 4.07 percent. That is inferior to almost every other expected cash return number in Table 1. Therefore, we try to avoid Japanese cash and overweight those markets in which cash equivalents provide a higher rate of return.

Implementation of the output of the currency forecast depends on the underlying portfolio. **Table 2** shows a portfolio with a benchmark index that invests in the United States, Japan, United Kingdom, Germany, France, Canada, and others. Seventy-five percent of the benchmark index is stated in U.S. currency and the remaining 25 percent in other currencies. The actual underlying portfolio is presumed to be overweighted in German securities and underweighted in U.S. securities. Thus, the underlying portfolio, prior to any currency adjustments, is posi-

tioned against the U.S. dollar, yen, and pound and for the deutsche mark. The active or actual cash exposure in the portfolio reveals that the portfolio is not completely invested in risky assets: Cash is being held primarily in U.S. cash equivalents. Currency hedging, which is a zero-sum game, is used to achieve the desired exposures based on expected cash returns in dollars. The combination of the active asset exposure, the active cash position, and currency hedging equals the active currency exposure.

The forward market can be used to achieve the desired currency exposure. For example, to achieve an active currency exposure of –5.3 percent to the yen, we hedged into the dollar and out of the deutsche mark, franc, and other currencies.

An interesting effect of separating the cash decision from the risky asset decision is that the local market return premium (the risk premium) becomes the focal point of the optimization of risky assets. The focal point involves making decisions about which countries to over- or underweight. In making the risky asset decision, an additional complexity arises at the global level. Risk is a relative concept;

Figure 4. U.S. Cents Per 100 Yen Exchange Rate, Actual and Equilibrium Bands, 1973–91

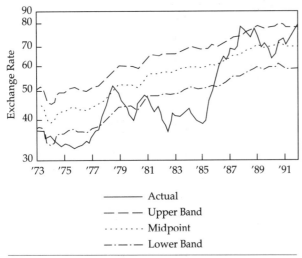

——— Actual
– – – Upper Band
········ Midpoint
–·–·– Lower Band

Source: Brinson Partners, Inc.

Note: Actual is quarter-end through fourth quarter 1991.

Table 1. The Currency Decision

Country	Expected Local Currency Rate Return	Expected Exchange Rate Return	Expected Cash Return in Dollars
Australia	8.25%	4.36%	3.54%
Canada	7.22	–1.02	6.13
France	8.58	–2.47	5.90
Germany	7.62	–1.98	5.48
Japan	5.37	–1.23	4.07
Netherlands	7.68	–1.20	6.33
United Kingdom	9.28	–4.58	4.28
United States	5.53	0.00	5.53

Source: Brinson Partners, Inc.

Note: Annualized five-year returns.

Table 2. Global Securities Currency Exposure

Currency	Benchmark Index[a]	Active Asset Exposure	+	Active Cash Exposure	+	Currency Hedging	=	Active Currency Exposure
United States	75.0%	−5.0%		10.1%		1.8%		6.9%
Japan	10.8	−6.2		0.4		0.6		−5.3
United Kingdom	3.9	−2.1		0.0		−0.6		−2.6
Germany	2.7	2.3		0.0		−1.0		1.3
France	1.9	0.9		0.0		−0.8		0.1
Canada	1.4	0.2		0.0		0.9		1.0
Others	4.3	−0.6		0.0		−0.9		−1.4
	100.0	−10.5		10.5		0.0		0.0

Source: Brinson Partners, Inc.

Note: Columns may not sum because of rounding.

[a]Benchmark: 67.0 percent total equity, 28.0 percent total bond, and 5.0 percent cash.

some context is required to gauge its meaning. In a global framework, the issue of what constitutes risk changes. If the focus is an individual country, the risk measure might be the standard deviation of the particular asset or asset class or it might involve the covariance between the asset in that country and other assets in that country. At the global level, risk for an asset class in a given country is widely defined relative to the covariance of the asset class with other global asset classes, all converted into the currency of the asset class of interest. This assumes that local currency investors are the primary determinants of the local asset class risk premium and that they put the asset class in a global portfolio context when attempting to assess the risk premium the asset class should pay.

Table 3 shows a set of expected return premiums for different markets. For Australia, for example, the expected local market return premium is 5.72 percent. This figure is then compared to a required local market return premium of 5.09 percent, which we think should exist in "equilibrium." The excess return opportunity, then, is 0.63 percent. **Table 4** illustrates an actual portfolio strategy that could be derived from global equity valuation, as in Table 3, and a similar table for global bond valuations. The guiding principle is to overweight the country markets with the highest excess returns.

Table 3. Global Equity Valuations

Market	Expected Local Market Return Premium	Required Local Market Return Premium	Excess Return
Australia	5.72%	5.09%	0.63%
Canada	0.03	4.42	−4.49
France	−4.27	5.11	−9.38
Germany	0.39	5.12	−4.73
Japan	−4.81	3.78	−8.59
Netherlands	1.87	4.54	−2.67
United Kingdom	1.35	4.88	−3.53
United States	0.08	4.36	−4.28
S&P 500 Market index	−1.59	4.40	−5.99

Source: Brinson Partners, Inc.

Table 4. Global Securities Portfolio
(base currency: U.S. dollar)

Item	Normal Policy	Current Strategy	Over-/ Underweight
Global equity	67.0%	19.5%	−47.5%
United States	50.0	15.0	−35.0
Non-U.S.	17.0	4.5	−12.5
Japan	7.4	1.0	−6.4
United Kingdom	3.1	1.1	−2.0
Germany	1.2	0.5	−0.7
France	1.1	0.3	−0.8
Other	4.2	1.6	−2.6
Global bonds	28.0	65.0	37.0
United States	20.0	50.0	30.0
Non-U.S.	8.0	15.0	7.0
Japan	3.0	3.5	0.5
United Kingdom	0.9	0.8	−0.1
Germany	1.5	4.4	2.9
France	0.9	2.5	1.6
Other	1.7	3.8	2.1
Cash	5.0	15.5	10.5
	100.0	100.0	0.0

Source: Brinson Partners, Inc.

Conclusion

Economic data can be used in constructing a global portfolio to derive an improved estimate of intrinsic value that can be compared to market price. This exercise is a little harder to do globally, but basically it uses the same kinds of factors that are used in domestic analysis. Global aggregate economic output determines the returns available for all investors, whether human capital or investment capital. Finally, in portfolio construction, the currency decision must be framed in a separate decision structure, and the risky asset decision must be framed in the context of the currency decision.

Question and Answer Session

Jeffrey J. Diermeier, CFA

Question: Is the main purpose of investing globally asset diversification?

Diermeier: By investing in common stocks or bonds around the globe, you avoid placing all your eggs in the basket of U.S. companies' abilities to grow domestically and externally via their foreign divisions. You might also want a direct participation in some other economies with natural endowments differing from those of the United States. At a given point in time, some investments may be more attractive than others.

Diversification is like a hedge. It is a trade-off between expected return and the risk of putting all your money in a single country. That is the classic portfolio-building paradigm. I cannot say why an investor chooses to trade off some expectation of risky return against diversifying into a pool of assets that will provide stability. For those managing fiduciary assets, this is a won-derful way to diversify against some very crucial variables that can dominate portfolio performance for a long period of time.

Question: Given the political and economic problems that exist outside the United States today, where does the world economy stand in the economic cycle?

Diermeier: We believe equity markets around the globe are too high. This is true of Japan, where the bubble has burst and the market is now in the process of unraveling. We do not see the unraveling stopping until Nikkei gets closer to 13,000 or 15,000; currently it is at 19,000. Europe poses some challenges, but we have some attractive valuations in several countries. Some nice real returns are available in fixed-income securities on a worldwide basis. Yet we are aware of the inflation risks, given the social demands in the United States and some other economies. Nevertheless, we are skewed more toward fixed-income securities to capture lower rates of inflation and skewed away from the higher prices that exist in some common stocks.

Question: You indicated that capital income in Japan is small relative to what is going on in that economy. How did the market stay up so long under those conditions?

Diermeier: The way the level held up in Japan is an enigma. It might be attributable to an illusion of low risk created by the authorities. If any risky market carries the impression that it is risk-less, a bubble will be built. Japan had a bubble market because many investors did not believe any risk existed there. Therefore, the market divorced itself from the economic realities. Now investors have the problem of dealing with a market that must feed on the economic realities.

Developing a Recommendation for a Global Portfolio

Charles I. Clough, Jr., CFA
Chief Investment Strategist
Merrill Lynch & Co.

Any set of disciplines a financial analyst uses to drive a global portfolio has to be designed to recognize change. Traditional approaches can provide a sense of intellectual complacency, particularly at important turning points in economic and financial market behavior. Missing those turning points can lead to underperformance.

The purpose of this presentation is not to bring another quantitative valuation model to the table or describe in detail how Merrill Lynch designs global portfolios, but rather to discuss the principles we use in investing across markets, and for that matter, in investing within a single market. Merrill Lynch, like most organizations, has the capability to build some fairly complicated models. Unfortunately, the more complicated the analysis, the more likely it is to miss the forest for the trees.

Any set of disciplines used to drive a global portfolio has to be designed to recognize change. Traditional approaches based simply on trend growth rate and interest rate levels often provide a sense of intellectual complacency, particularly at important turning points in economic and financial market behavior. Missing those turning points can lead to underperformance.

Anticipating Change in Fundamental Trends

We use a number of important principles in designing a global investment portfolio. First is the need to understand what we do not know. Not only are the more traditional domestic inputs of investment activity, such as yield curve behavior and credit market activity, important to global decision making but also currency values and different accounting conventions must be considered. It is easy to extrapolate all the domestic ambiguities and uncertainties. Second is the need to assess where important secular changes may have occurred that could accelerate or decelerate a region's growth, where the valuation formulas, especially the inputs, might be wrong.

Change always occurs at the margin, and as recent events in Latin America and China suggest, it can be profound. Third is the need for a series of disciplines to help determine where the consensus might be wrong. If consensus estimates about earnings, growth rates, risk premiums, and so forth are pumped into the discipline, the models produce consensus output and, probably, subpar returns.

Two experiences I had as a portfolio manager suggest reasons for skepticism about popular types of analysis—particularly unidimensional analysis, such as simple dividend discount modeling—when important changes are afoot. By early 1979, valuation formulas or dividend discount models during the late stages of the energy boom of the 1970s suggested underweighting energy stocks. The growth rate and earnings estimates were based on the experience investors had viewing the industry over the postwar period. By March 1979, the oil service stocks and many international and domestic integrated stocks were emerging as extremely overvalued on our internal valuation models. As events turned out, two-thirds of the rise in the sector's stock prices still lay ahead. The stocks did not peak until almost 18 months later. Because of the unprecedented rise in energy prices, the earnings momentum dynamic carried earnings, profit margins, and stock market valuations much higher than historical patterns. The models could not predict change, and something had changed.

The second event was in 1985, at the bottom of the paper stock price cycle. As the industry moved out of recession, our valuation model indicated that on the basis of its price–earnings ratio (P/E), even when the measure was based on peak earnings and peak returns on investment in a future time frame, one particular container board company's stock was fairly valued. (Cyclical stocks tend to rise sharply at the beginning of their cycles. They will take a big jump off their lows and appear to have already discounted the cycle, even though much of the earnings gains lie ahead). Despite the appearance of overvaluation, the stock subsequently increased in price nearly 10 times. It had moved ahead from $10 to $28 but then moved to more than $200 a share on the then-outstanding stock. The company's balance sheet was highly leveraged, so the pricing and leverage dynamics combined to carry nominal earnings up dramatically. Again, something had changed.

In international investing, the possibility of change increases exponentially. At Merrill Lynch, domestic and international portfolio strategy is based on a number of complementary observations:

■ *Markets are rational.* This is true even though they can sustain abnormally high or low P/Es or the appearance of overvaluation or undervaluation for extended periods of time. This is the basis by which securities markets, particularly equity markets, direct capital flows. High risk premiums or low risk premiums are a way of controlling capital flows. A combination of value, liquidity, and earnings momentum techniques is used to attempt to capture the dynamic element of change and to determine what is happening in industries and in markets to weave an understanding of economic and industry dynamics. A portfolio is then designed around those disciplines.

■ *Some inputs must be conjectural rather than quantitative.* Conjectural judgments are necessary and often are difficult to put into quantitative terms. In 1987, for example, the Japanese central bank engineered a dramatic decline in the cost of capital as part of a coordinated central bank policy of dollar support. That move unleashed a torrent of liquidity into the Japanese real estate and stock markets, creating a speculative explosion in prices and a subsequent bust (which is still working itself out). These markets were substantially overvalued long before they peaked, both in time and levels. Their peaks occurred when market liquidity began to deteriorate, but by that time they had gone well beyond levels anyone thought possible. Being underweight in Japan hurt a diversified international portfolio dramatically for a long period of time. Liquidity, if it is powerful and long lasting, can drive both valuation and themes to excess. More important is to recognize when those forces have peaked. Recognizing that markets are overvalued simply is not enough.

■ *We look at markets from a top-down and bottom-up perspective simultaneously.* This is particularly true

if a major international investment theme is emerging across several markets. The practice is important in dealing with smaller markets, such as Switzerland or Malaysia, in which capitalization constraints limit the ability to diversify within the market. Portfolio representation in a particular market may not be based on that market's valuation parameters but on a theme, such as technology or infrastructure, that is highly represented in that market.

■ *In the 1990s, most of the world's growth will occur outside the industrialized nations.* Trends in demography and in debt suggest growing deflationary patterns will hinder earnings in many large equity markets. Currently, Merrill Lynch's global portfolios are overweighted in Hong Kong, Latin America, and to a lesser extent, France, and they are underweighted in Japan, Germany, and some of the smaller Asian markets.

■ *Evidence suggests that a major worldwide credit contraction is under way.* This will affect economic growth, bank rates, bond yields, and P/Es in much of the industrialized world. Credit cycles have peaked almost everywhere. Bank deposit rates have declined to surprisingly low levels in North America. If the debt deflation persists, returns to household deposits will fall to low levels—with the United States in the lead—and remain low in most industrialized nations throughout much of the decade.

■ *The dollar is likely to be a strong currency in this credit contraction.* At the moment, it is weak against those European Monetary System currencies tied to the deutsche mark, where currency rates are at stranglehold levels. The dollar, however, is not being inflated. More fairly stated, the deutsche mark is strong rather than the dollar is weak. In fact, the absence of domestic credit expansion could be the source of a dollar shortage in the 1990s. The United States is further along the declining phase of the credit curve than most other nations, and the availability of dollar liquidity in the world is shrinking, leaving us somewhat overweighted in the U.S. market in global portfolios. By 1993, recovery cycles are likely to emerge in the rest of the industrialized world, particularly Europe. Recovery is already somewhat visible in North America, but in Japan, Europe, and other countries, economies are still weakening. The upcoming cycle, however, will be tame by postwar period standards. The demographics of aging are beginning to play a major role in all industrialized nations, and interest rates will probably continue to decline in the 1990s as in the 1980s. Consequently, the 1990s will bring lower financial market returns and even lower cash returns than the 1980s.

■ *By the middle of the decade, capital will flow to*

obvious places. These include Eastern Europe, Latin America, India, and China. P/Es in most industrialized stock markets will be at higher levels because credit will not be used speculatively, freeing up domestic savings for investment capital. Capital will flow to developing areas at astonishingly low costs relative to the yields at the long end of the yield curves in most industrialized nations.

Money Supply and a Credit Contraction

Slower rates of growth in borrowing will affect the way money grows in all industrialized nations. The United States is a prime example, but the same monetary patterns are emerging in other economies. Declining worldwide money growth will affect valuation and how equities and fixed-income instruments will be priced. The narrow U.S. monetary aggregates are up. M1 is up 12 percent year-on-year. In contrast, as **Figure 1** shows, M3 is contracting. In fact, the year-on-year growth of M3 is at the lowest level ever. M3 is the critical monetary aggregate because (1) it eliminates the distortions that arise as the result of people changing the way they hold deposits, and (2) it measures the totality of the banking system's deposit base. To transaction balances in M1, M3 adds small-time deposits that are in M2. Most international money supply measures basically break down the same way. To M2, M3 adds overnight repos, Eurodollar term deposits, and large time deposits. Those are the deposits for which banks must aggressively bid. To increase its total deposit base, or the liability side of its balance sheet, a bank must aggressively expand its M3-type deposits. That is a signal that a real credit upcycle is beginning. Currently, the credit cycles in the United States and other nations are still headed the other way.

In the United States, a banking system consolidation process is under way. When Manufacturers Hanover and Chemical merged, for example, a num-ber of events occurred in New York. First, a headquarters building and its related real estate proved excessive. Branch offices were closed and employment fell, but those were rather superficial events. Most important was the banking system's downsizing of its balance sheet. The reason the two banks had to merge was that the New York metropolitan area did not produce enough loans or assets to support the size of the banking system that had evolved there. When the banks stopped lending to build excessive real estate, they were forced to downsize their assets and liquidate liabilities.

This is happening globally as well. In Canada, for example, some banks are holding assets of lesser value than they think. Likewise, in the United Kingdom and Japan, as real estate assets shrink, so do the banks' liabilities, which are primarily household deposits.

The banking system is consolidating because the demand for credit is not likely to grow much in the future. The United States has had a production bounce in the economy that indicates it will lead to expansion, but as **Figure 2** shows, that is not happening in credit. In a credit contraction, the broad money supply does not grow much. Before earlier upcycles, M3 grew faster than M1 or M2. Now, not only is M3 the slowest growing aggregate but it also is at the lowest rate of growth ever. Even though the economy appears to be several months into an expansion, money and credit are still not growing much.

A second characteristic of a credit contraction is that nominal income growth is not rapid. U.S. nominal disposable income grew only 3 percent in 1991—the slowest rate since 1960. The two-year moving average for disposable income growth, shown in **Figure 3**, has declined to less than 6 percent. The last time the Federal Reserve Board reduced the discount rate from 4.5 percent to 3.5 percent, which probably kicked off this credit cycle, was in 1930. Thus, this

Figure 1. U.S. Broad Money Supply (M3), 1961–91
(year-to-year percent change)

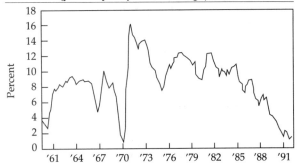

Source: Federal Reserve System.

Figure 2. U.S. Private Nonfinancial Debt, 1956–91
(year-to-year percent change)

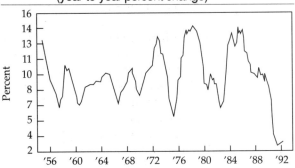

Source: Federal Reserve System.

Figure 3. U.S. Nominal Disposable Income, 1962–91
(year-to-year percent change, two-year
moving average)

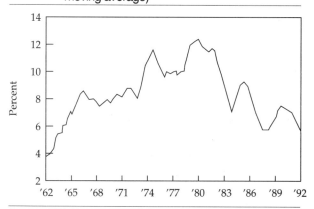

Source: U.S. Department of Commerce, Bureau of Economic Analysis.

recession has produced record-low interest rates, record-low nominal activity, and record-low short-term yields.

Demographic Trends and Labor Costs

Slow labor force growth may lead long-term interest rates lower in the 1990s in the industrialized world. How the demographic trends in the United States affect the labor force and employment is shown in **Figure 4**. Similar trends are found in Japan, the United Kingdom, and many other Western European nations. Most populations are becoming older, and growth rates are declining, particularly in Western Europe.

Employment growth is sluggish in this cycle because demand for labor is in a secular decline. The corporate sector is doing something perfectly rational: Companies are downsizing their need for labor because labor will become less available in the 1990s and because labor cost is exorbitant.

According to most demographic studies, U.S. labor force growth will slow to somewhere between 0.5 percent and 1 percent a year in the 1990s, which is down from 1.75 percent in the 1980s and 2.75 percent in the 1970s. Labor force growth is declining in Europe. Some observers have suggested this may lead to labor shortages in the 1990s. Business will bid up the price of labor, and a cost-push form of inflation will develop, especially with all the social pressures for universally available health care and higher retirement costs for an aging work force. History suggests a different scenario may evolve. As Figure 4 shows, yields tend to follow demographics with a notable lag, and demographics and credit cycles appear to be positively correlated.

Population growth will be slow not only in the

United States but also in other industrialized nations. The labor force has already absorbed the postwar baby boomers, their offspring, and a high percentage of women. If demand for consumer goods and services grows correspondingly more slowly, the extra airport, office, and mall space that has been built will take longer to be absorbed. Concerns are mounting that even Hong Kong's long-anticipated airport may be a white elephant. Personal employment growth is slow because many service industries are overstaffed. Nominal income and spending growth will both slow. Economics may be systemically slower in the industrialized world because fewer people are entering the borrowing and spending times of their lives.

Population dynamics may be playing a role in credit cycles around the world. If so, corporations will shift back from heavy use of labor to greater emphasis on capital. Labor has already become so expensive that corporations have every incentive to substitute capital for labor. **Figure 5** shows trends in U.S. manufacturing labor compensation per hour relative to output per hour—unit labor costs stated crudely. This ratio moved up sharply in the 1970s

Figure 4. U.S. Labor Force Growth, 1952–91
(year-to-year percent change, two-year
moving average)

Total Labor Force Growth and Treasury Yields

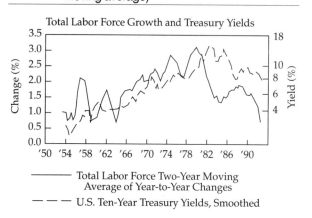

———— Total Labor Force Two-Year Moving
Average of Year-to-Year Changes

— — — U.S. Ten-Year Treasury Yields, Smoothed

Two-Year Moving Average of the
Year-to-Year Labor Force Growth Rate

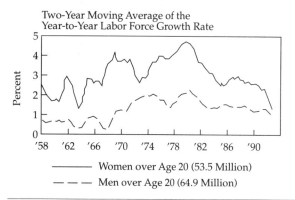

———— Women over Age 20 (53.5 Million)

— — — Men over Age 20 (64.9 Million)

Source: U.S. Department of Labor, Bureau of Labor Statistics.

Figure 5. Unit Labor Cost, U.S. Manufacturing Sector, 1948–90
(ratio of compensation per hour to output per hour)

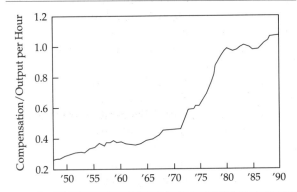

Source: U.S. Department of Labor, Bureau of Labor Statistics.

and 1980s. As long as the manufacturing sector could pass those costs through in prices, the cost-push inflationary pattern fed on itself. Once the dollar became overvalued and U.S. manufacturers could not raise prices to cover higher labor costs, the manufacturing sector hit the wall. Massive cash flow deficits resulted, along with a long-term process of "restructuring" (reducing the labor component of costs).

The U.S. manufacturing sector has been fairly successful in controlling labor costs. Manufacturing employment declined during the 1980s, as shown in **Figure 6**. It peaked in the late 1970s, and during the longest peacetime expansion we have had on record, manufacturing employment declined 15 percent from its peak. General Motors, for example, has the capacity to manufacture 5.5 million automobiles, but it only sells 3 million. It is hemorrhaging cash at the rate of about $15 million a day. No matter how large your balance sheet, if you lose cash that fast, sooner or later you run out of it. So, Mr. Stempel has to close

Figure 6. Total Employment, U.S. Manufacturing Sector, 1948–90
(millions)

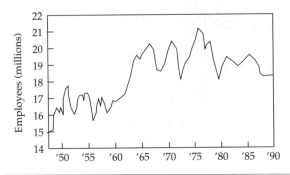

Source: U.S. Department of Labor, Bureau of Labor Statistics.

plants sooner than he thought. If he closes 21 plants, reportedly, 75,000 additional layoffs will take place. The growing trend around the world toward the establishment of trading blocs will only intensify pressures for greater productive efficiency, lower costs, and higher quality. The emergence of Europe and North America as regional trading blocs will create a great deal of redundant production capacity. This represents another change in investment equation inputs.

Figure 7 shows what is happening to labor costs in the services sector. Most advanced economies are service driven, and labor costs are still accelerating in that sector. The impending peak in U.S. service-sector employment **(Figure 8)** may be occurring in a number of economies. In the four largest services segments—finance, insurance, retail and wholesale trade, and defense—employment is contracting, which will probably slow the growth of the services labor force. As in manufacturing, service-sector businesses will make a more concentrated attempt to reduce the labor component of their costs—another change in economic inputs.

Figure 7. Unit Labor Cost, U.S. Services Sector, 1964–91
(ratio of weekly payroll index to output)

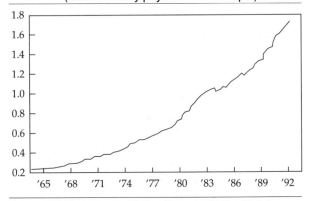

Source: U.S. Department of Labor, Bureau of Labor Statistics.

Credit Demands

An often-heard concern earlier this year was that as the economy starts to recover, private-sector credit demands would soar. The common perception is that heavy public-sector financing by the U.S. government will force higher interest rates. On the contrary, I believe long-term bond markets offer substantial value, not only in the United States but also around the world.

Again, using the United States as an example that can be extrapolated internationally, the total U.S. credit structure includes about $11 trillion of nonfi-

Figure 8. Total Employment, U.S. Services Sector, 1948–90
(millions)

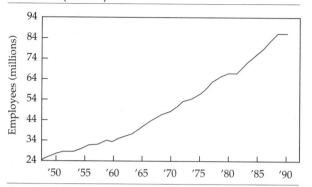

Source: U.S. Department of Labor, Bureau of Labor Statistics.

nancial debt, which is defined as debt outside the banking system. This debt, broken down by maturity, is shown in **Figure 9**. The economy's short-term debt, defined as M4 or liquidity, consists primarily of bank deposits and Treasury bills. The size of this type of debt—$5 trillion—shows the effect of a positive yield curve: A dynamically positive yield curve inhibits the creation of long-term debt and pulls more liquidity to the short end of the curve. This is also happening in other industrialized nations.

The vast bulk of the long-term credit in today's society consists of mortgage debt—loans used to fund real estate. Real estate developers in every industrialized country borrow more money than any other entity, including governments. In the process, they have created more than $4 trillion of mortgage credit in the United States.

The remaining debt amounts to about $2 trillion. About $400 billion, or 4 percent of the nation's credit structure, is long-term government debt, or 5- to 30-year paper. Although government debt is not a large component of the nation's debt, it is important because prices of other debt types, such as mortgages, are based on the long-term government yield. About $600 billion dollars represents long-term corporate debt—investment-grade and high-yield bonds. The remaining debt stock consists of various forms of personal debt—consumer installment credit, for example, which may not extend out more than a year, but the Federal Reserve data include it in the "other" category because these are not large debt aggregates.

Figure 9 presents an extrapolated picture of the banking system's balance sheet. M4 consists largely of banking system liabilities such as certificates of deposits, money funds, and guaranteed investment contracts sitting in life insurance companies. These liabilities are used to fund mortgage debt. If the financial sector cannot inflate real estate credit, it

cannot pay high returns on the deposits held by the household sector. If igniting a mortgage-driven real estate credit cycle proves impossible, credit growth will be very sluggish. Two-thirds of mortgage debt consists of one- to four-family home mortgages. These are great credit instruments to a fiduciary or investor because the household sector generally pays the rent on time. Default rates are low, and the duration or maturity of these credit instruments tends to be stable. Homeowners will not suddenly try to exchange 9 percent fixed-rate mortgages for adjustable rate mortgages. That is exactly what they should do, but unless interest rates collapse, people tend to hold onto their long-term mortgages. The problem is that we are not creating many new residential mortgages. The creation of residential credit is experiencing a sharp slowdown. The demographics are such that we are no longer inflating the housing stock in most of the industrialized world.

The large stock of commercial mortgages outstanding is what will give the U.S. banking and insurance sector, the Japanese banking system, and part of the Canadian and U.K. banking systems a run for their money in the next few years. Many of these

Figure 9. U.S. Debt, 2Q1991
(trillions of dollars)

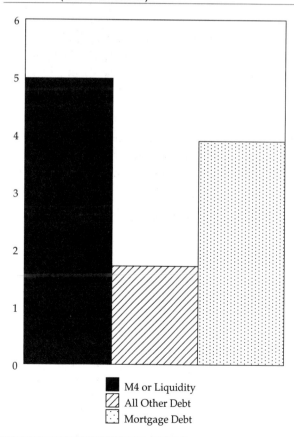

■ M4 or Liquidity
▨ All Other Debt
▒ Mortgage Debt

Source: Federal Reserve System, Flow of Funds.

are first mortgages on existing structures that may produce a cash flow; the lessees are actually paying the rent. As the leases on buildings built between 1982 and 1986 run out, however, those cash flows will start to collapse. Many current facilities are backed by single-payment, "bullet" mortgages that will mature between 1993 and 1996. Although carried on the books at full value in most instances, many of these mortgages will default. New leases are being written at rental rates that are fractions of the rates built into the original leases. In short, a lot of loan restructurings lie ahead. The "Canary Wharf" problem in London and Tokyo's real estate horror stories suggest that worldwide defaults are on the way.

The problems with commercial mortgage credit have been well chronicled. What is less understood is the impact of these defaults on the yield curve. As mortgages default or liquidate, the duration or maturity of the credit market shrinks. The value of long-term mortgage credit declines, and investors have trouble locking in duration or yield. The same event is unfolding in Japan and the United Kingdom. As leases run out, the value of the buildings and the underlying mortgages collapses. Not only will this continue to depress commercial mortgage activity but also it will force banks holding such mortgages to reduce the yield on their deposit liabilities. This is the downside of the credit cycle.

The volume of high-quality long-term corporate credit will similarly shrink if current trends persist. Of the $600 billion of corporate bonds currently outstanding, about 25 percent, or $166 billion, are likely to be called in 1992. Much of that will not be refunded in the long-term bond market because borrowing there is so expensive. Funding is cheaper in equities, in the commercial paper market, or along the five- to seven-year part of the curve. In a period of credit deflation, as banks reduce their funding rates, the yield curve will remain steeply positive. The fact that the bank rate fell below 3 percent is perfectly consistent with the beginning of a credit contraction. Lower rates of borrowing will likely translate into far lower rates paid on U.S. money market securities, and sooner or later, those abroad as well.

The Structure of Savings

Changing demographics also affect savings rates, as **Figure 10** shows. As the number of people between the ages of 40 and 64 rises as a percentage of the total adult population, the U.S. savings rate will start to rise. That is already beginning and is reflected in the dollar's stability in the face of a severe arbitrage

Figure 10. U.S. Savings Rate and the Proportion of the Population Likely to be Savers, 1959–99
(estimated)

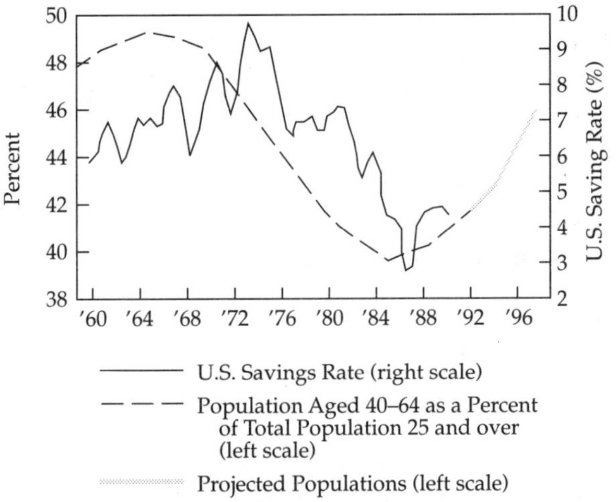

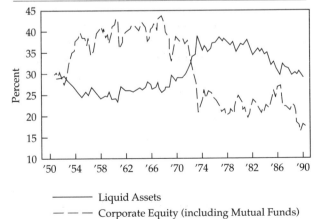

———— U.S. Savings Rate (right scale)

– – – Population Aged 40–64 as a Percent of Total Population 25 and over (left scale)

·········· Projected Populations (left scale)

Source: Federal Reserve System, Flow of Funds.

exchange rate discount, particularly with respect to the German mark. The U.S. bank rate is 3 percent, Germany's is 9 percent, and the dollar is no lower relative to the German currency than it was in 1988. That is only possible if we, as a nation, are throwing off excess savings.

The composition of household financial assets is changing, albeit slowly. Liquid assets as a percent of household financial assets are declining, as **Figure 11** shows. This implies that a major restructuring of the nation's savings pattern is under way. **Figure 12** suggests a migration from certificates of deposit to bonds and stocks is in an early stage. As of the third quarter of 1991, low percentages of household financial assets were still held in the forms of savings

Figure 11. U.S. Ownership of Equities as a Percent of Household Financial Assets, 1951–91

———— Liquid Assets

– – – Corporate Equity (including Mutual Funds)

Source: Federal Reserve System, Flow of Funds.

Figure 12. Securities as a Percent of Household Financial Assets, 1954–91

Sources: Federal Reserve System, Flow of Funds; Merrill Lynch Strategy.

Note: Securities included are savings; government, tax-exempt, and corporate bonds; equities; and mutual funds.

bonds, government bonds, tax-exempt bonds, equities, and mutual funds. **Figure 13** shows that despite record-low money market rates, the household sector is still increasing its holdings of money-fund-type assets such as insurance policies and guaranteed investment contracts. Changing liquidity preferences is a long-term process. So long as the household sector insists on holding its assets at the 90-day bank rate and the banking system faces lower credit demands, the rate paid on household deposits will continue to fall. In the 1990s, bank rates should be astonishingly low. Eventually, that will force savers out on the yield curve and into equities, an event that could change the long-term valuation parameters characterizing most of the world's equity markets during the postwar period.

Figure 13. The "Other Financial Assets" Category as a Percent of U.S. Household Financial Assets

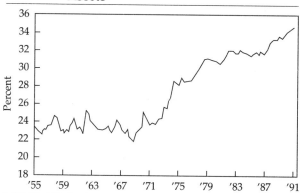

Sources: Federal Reserve System, Flow of Funds; Merrill Lynch Strategy.

Note: Other financial assets include private life insurance and pension reserves (insured and noninsured), government insurance, and miscellaneous financial assets.

Two forms of credit can grow. One is commercial and industrial loans—working-capital lending—which in the United States amounts to about $280 billion. The other is consumer installment credit, which is now $600 billion. Consumers have been liquidating credit for the first time in history during this recession, but it could pick up a little in 1993. So about $900 billion of credit might grow. Mortgages outstanding total $4 trillion. Without a real estate inflation, whether it is based on an inflating value of the housing stock or a commercial credit cycle, no credit expansion is likely to be significant enough to absorb the credit capacity in the banking system.

The banking and insurance sectors will be shrinking on three continents. As that happens, these institutions must liquidate their liabilities. This should lead to very low bank rates through the 1990s, first in the United States and eventually in Europe and Japan. Short-term notes' interest rates may bounce a bit as production gains in the middle of 1992, but beyond that bounce, rates will settle at much lower levels. The long end of the curve will have to take care of itself. That will take a while longer simply because of all the indigenous fears in the minds of investors, from government deficits to inflation, but the economics we see will clearly sustain downward pressure on the 90-day bank rate.

Future Issues

The equity markets of the world face three risks. The first is that central banks will overstay tight credit policies. Again, in a domestic credit contraction, tight central bank policies are neither likely nor helpful. **Figure 14** illustrates an indicator of the banking system's balance sheet that correlates fairly well with stock prices. This indicator plots the ratio of nonborrowed reserves plus extended credit to required reserves on a 13-week rate-of-change basis. When the ratio moves up, banking system liquidity is increasing, and the result is generally a bottom in equity prices. The last one was on November 19, 1991. A fall in the indicator would be a cause for concern about a sharper market correction, but as the bottom panel of Figure 14 suggests, bank liquidity is picking up systemically.

The second risk is the possibility of a trade war with Europe, Japan, or the Southeast Asian "tiger" economies. World capital markets probably would not like that. A trade war could be a serious event because all industrialized nations are leveraged, and a trade war would impede the flow of capital.

The third risk for the financial markets is bad fiscal policy, a possibility that must be taken seri-

Figure 14. Bank Liquidity and Stock Prices, 1982–91

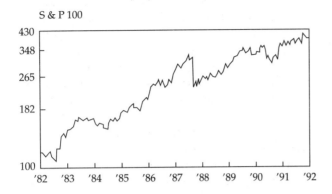

S & P 100

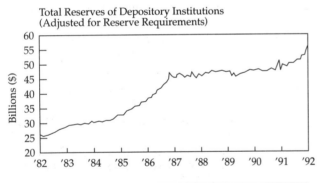

Nonborrowed Reserves and
Extended Credit/Required Reserves
(13-week Rate of Change)

Total Reserves of Depository Institutions
(Adjusted for Reserve Requirements)

Source: Federal Reserve System, Release H.3.

Figure 15. U.S. Economic Rate of Change and Bank Reserves, 1959–91
(year-to-year percent change)

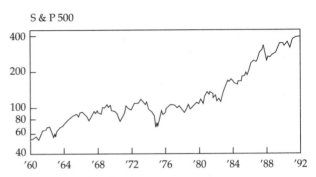

S & P 500

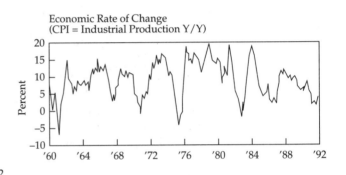

Economic Rate of Change
(CPI = Industrial Production Y/Y)

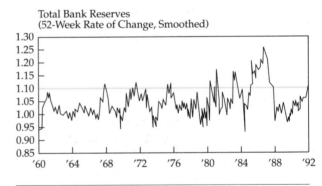

Total Bank Reserves
(52-Week Rate of Change, Smoothed)

Sources: Federal Reserve System; Standard & Poor's; Merrill Lynch Investment Strategy.

ously in an election year. A constituency for a major effort to expand public-sector deficits has not surfaced as yet, however.

A modest cyclical expansion appears to be under way in the United States. **Figure 15** shows that bank reserves are starting to expand, which usually precedes a rise in spending and production. The economic rate of change is the consumer price index multiplied by industrial production. Industrial production has bottomed, and so our equity strategy, not only domestically but around the world, is becoming more focused on companies that are tied to the level of economic activity.

Liquidity as a Determinant of Equity Exposure

On a worldwide basis, liquidity available to the financial markets peaked in the late 1980s and has been at least stable since then. No new sustained peaks in the world equity index will occur without liquidity growth (see **Figure 16**). The reason for this is shown in **Figure 17**, which shows the pattern of real broad money supply growth in four of the major G-7 countries with large capital markets. The broad money supply in Japan is defined as M2 plus certificates of deposits; in the United Kingdom, it is M4; and in Germany and the United States, it is M3. The worldwide pattern has been one of consistent deceleration in inflation-adjusted money supply growth. One

Figure 16. World Equity Index, 1978–91

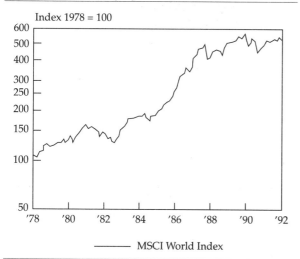

Index 1978 = 100

—— MSCI World Index

Source: Morgan Stanley Capital International World Index.

reason is that, on a worldwide basis, economies are not creating liquidity. Liquidity builds when somebody borrows, and very little of that is happening anywhere. At the same time, however, the economies are absorbing very little liquidity because no one is spending. So we are in a stalemate. Yield curves, on balance, are becoming positive.

As borrowing slows, the world appears to be moving toward a systematically positive yield curve. **Figure 18** illustrates the ratio of the long-term government bond yield to the three-month Eurocurrency rate. Each market is weighted by the size of its bank deposits. Gradually, positive yield curves are

Figure 17. Real Broad Money Growth and Industrial Production, Four G-7 Countries, 1977–91
(year-to-year percent change)

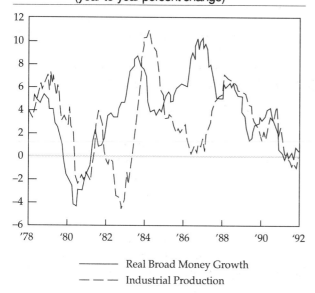

—— Real Broad Money Growth
– – – Industrial Production

Source: Federal Reserve Board.

being reestablished everywhere. Germany is the laggard because the Bundesbank has to deal with the one-shot blip in the Germany money supply stemming from reunification. The credit cycle in Japan is not too far behind that of the United States. The world will see lower growth and less inflation in the 1990s in most of the industrialized economies. Many economies are facing the same slowing demographic patterns as the United States. They are also burdened with an overbuilt services sector and excess employment. The positive in all of this is that a lot of liquidity is parked at the short end of the yield curve in all markets, and that tendency is being exacerbated in Germany.

The concern a year ago was that the Japanese would sell their foreign bonds and bring home the money to forestall a real estate deflation. The Japanese have been liquidating their holdings of U.S. Treasury bonds since 1986, and now 88 percent of the Treasury's debt is held domestically, largely because U.S. domestic savings rates have been picking up for the past several years. Would Somitono Bank sell its last remaining dollar-earning asset to lend to a real estate developer in Tokyo or to try to bail somebody out? I doubt it. In fact, the trade numbers imply that the Bank of Japan is trying to let that nation's credit deflation down easy. An aggressive liquidation of dollar bonds on the part of Japanese banking institutions is highly unlikely.

In the meantime, the Japanese household sector sits on a vast stock of savings, which Japan is starting to export again. Japan is running an $85 billion current account surplus and continues to export capital. The difference is that the United States is also a capital exporter for the first time in decades. That is

Figure 18. Ratio of Long-Term Government Bond Yield to the Three-Month Eurocurrency Rate, 1977–91

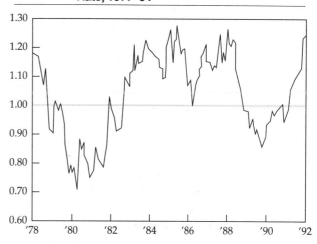

Source: Federal Reserve Board.

not likely if we are importing it.

These dominant changes in the use of money and credit will have a dramatic effect on national growth rates and capital flows and on how well traditional valuation models work. The cost of capital world-wide is falling because virtually all the industrialized nations are experiencing the downside of the great postwar real estate credit cycles. In the final analysis, real estate drives credit. As we go into the 1990s, the bank rate will continue to fall, with cyclical variations, in most industrialized nations.

The final question is whether developing world credit needs will overwhelm world credit markets. We think not. As the industrialized nations stem the speculative use of borrowing, capital will be available for those parts of the world that need it. Even though the focus of these investment flows will be on decade-long investment patterns, capital should be available at astonishingly low rates.

Capital cycles that provide investment for building up an underdeveloped nation's industrial stock or an investment base usually are accompanied by low capital costs. Cycles dominated by speculative capital uses or that are consumption based—used to build casinos or golf courses—are characterized by high capital costs.

Outlook for the Financial Markets

In designing a global portfolio with state-of-the-art valuation and interest rate markets, we monitor the relationship of broad money growth to industrial production in various economies. The strong markets tend to be liquidity driven; domestic money supplies are growing more rapidly than industrial production. The United States is the only industrialized nation beginning to rebuild liquidity. We believe modest credit expansion and recovery is under way, and the recovery is unlikely to be strong enough to build inflationary pressures into the system.

Broad money growth in the United Kingdom still seems to be decelerating. Industrial production is not growing; it has only stopped declining. Japan seems to be in a state of virtual liquidity collapse. It is in the process of unwinding several heavy inflationary bubbles in several sectors. One is the securities markets. Another is real estate, which became terribly overvalued. Even the industrial stock became overbuilt. A tremendous boom took place in industrial capital spending, to a large extent in sunset industries, such as automobiles and consumer electronics, and that cycle is unwinding as well. Borrowing is now collapsing, and Japan's banking system is in the process of downsizing.

Germany is almost comatose. The Bundesbank is trying to offset the money supply growth caused by reunification, but industrial production is starting to decline, and the real money supply is beginning to pick up. A decline in interest rates and an increase in money supply should stabilize the stock market, perhaps later in 1992.

The U.S. equity markets are overvalued relative to bonds and undervalued relative to cash, and that will continue to be the real investment enigma of the 1990s. This pattern will soon be repeated in other nations. The equity markets will look overvalued relative to the fixed-income side because bonds are discounting such possibilities as inflation and excessive credit demands, which we doubt will happen. The cash rate will stay low if we encourage world-wide credit contracts. In the long run, low cash rates would probably drive stock markets to the point that P/Es will begin to look uncomfortably high. Stock markets will not fit the patterns of the past 30 years, because that period captured a major increase in the use of credit to power economic cycles and asset inflation. Before the expansion was far along, some nonmarket asset was inflating and driving liquidity out of the financial markets.

The stock markets will probably start to discount a declining cost of capital, and high P/Es will become more common. The markets would be very rational in doing this. They are pricing down the cost of capital, especially for those sectors of the economy that require investment. The economic cycles in the 1990s will be investment driven, and your guess is as good as mine as to where that investment will flow.

The Japanese stock market is coming closer to a better valuation pattern as the central bank brings the bank rate down. Credit deflations are tricky; where they will bottom out is hard to predict. We would rather see Japanese stocks go fully undervalued before we step back in.

The model for the U.K.'s stock market is neutral. Before we will increase our U.K. weightings, interest rates will have to fall or the money supply expand, suggesting a coming expansion. Germany's market is still overvalued because yields are very high. We would rather stay on the fixed-income side of most European capital markets right now. Once we see clear signs of substantial economic weakness, those markets will probably move toward undervaluation. Currently, France looks like the best value. It has artificially high rates because they have to stay in line with Germany's rates. Once rates decline, market opportunities should improve in Japan, Spain, and Hong Kong. The most interesting part of the world is southern Asia, although those markets also entail risks, many of which are political.

Conclusion

Bank rates are likely to be in systemic decline throughout the world in the 1990s, which will change the way historic valuation models work. The U.S. market might see a temporary bounce at the short end of the curve, but borrowing or spending will probably not be sufficient to allow the banks to use their credit capacity, so they are unlikely to bid aggressively for deposits. In two or three years, the 90-day certificate of deposit may become extinct. It is a creature of the 1970s, when banks were given the flexibility to expand their balance sheets by building deposit liabilities because a major, once-in-a-lifetime credit cycle was under way.

The psychology of banking is changing. With low bank rates in one industrialized nation after another, the correct investment strategy will be to shift to long-term financial assets in these countries. At the margin, bonds may currently offer better value than stocks. In recovering economies, particularly in the United States, we lean modestly toward stocks because of the outlook for higher earnings in 1993. Stocks will appear systemically overvalued as long as the credit cycle is unwinding.

Question and Answer Session

Charles I. Clough, Jr., CFA

Question: Please comment on immigration in the United States and capital movements in Europe.

Clough: Immigration is remarkably easy to analyze. In the United States, its growth might be peaking. In the 1980s, we had tremendous immigration flows, on a smaller base, largely from Hispanic and Asiatic nations. Ironically, with Mexico beginning to advance and Latin America beginning to change, a reversal of flight capital has begun. We may be overestimating the effect of immigration.

Internationally, capital flows must be kept open. They should not be artificially shut off, because that would create shocks that could get out of control. A year ago, I was bearish on Eastern Europe and the Soviet Union because many estimates about capital flows were guesses. Hundreds of billions of dollars were supposedly going to flow to Eastern Europe once it opened up. Those estimates were specious. Since then, civil wars have erupted, and we are learning how difficult a turnaround in that part of the world is. So Eastern Europe is not a very hospitable place for capital, although that situation might be bottoming. If they can settle their ethnic rivalries, capital might move very quickly into that part of the world.

Question: What is the flavor of the stock market in the environment you described?

Clough: Since the 1987 crash, the market has been changing from a consumption-driven to an investment-driven market. The current investment cycle substitutes low-cost capital and technology for labor.

The cyclical expansion will have several themes. The first theme is restructuring, mainly in the transportation sector among truckers, railroads, and airlines and in some heavy-duty truck and auto parts industries. Mack and Navistar, for example, are shadows of their former selves. The trucking industry has been underreplacing its fleet for almost five years now, and new Environmental Protection Agency emission guidelines are due. Such stocks as PACCAR and Cummins Engine have experienced a long down cycle. That marketplace has no Japanese exposure at all; U.S. firms have essentially priced them out of it. We are looking for a capital cycle in that industry.

The second theme is technology. After a giant rally in technology during 1991, many of these stocks became overvalued. Computer manufacturing is now a mature business, but technology is not computers any more. With open systems and tremendous ex-

cess capacity, computer manufacturing margins will continue to collapse. The opportunities are in services and software development.

Third is an eclectic distribution theme. The question of growth as opposed to value might miss the point. The old consumer growth stocks, such as drugs and foods, are not overvalued. Their relative multiples are not bad; they are not that high relative to the earnings and return on equity they have created. What is high are the profit margins. In a number of industries, particularly the nondurable sector, new companies and competition will be taking potshots at those margins throughout the 1990s. In food or nondurable industries, I would rather control the shelf space than protect a brand franchise. Perhaps the food retailers could be interesting. I favor investing in the point of distribution, whether it is a retail food chain or a strong, well-managed hospital or nursing home chain. Drug and hospital care or food and household product profit margins may not migrate to the point of delivery. These tend to be cyclical types of industries. The question for the old consumer growth stocks is this: Can they protect their profit margins?

Self-Evaluation Examination

1. *Explain* why Bostian views forecasting as both a science and an art.

2. *Identify* the three major risks in economic forecasting, according to Bostian.

3. According to Bostian, rate of change is a good method for expressing a discipline for forecasting the economic cycle.
   a. True.
   b. False.

4. *List* three major differences between the Bostian Macro-Economic Index and the federal government's Leading Economic Indicators.

5. Bostian emphasizes making the domestic forecast first and then making changes on the basis of international considerations.
   a. True.
   b. False.

6. According to McNees, the forecast period is the most important factor underlying the variability of forecast errors.
   a. True.
   b. False.

7. *List* at least three reasons forecast accuracy has improved over time.

8. For most economic variables, forecasters can beat statistical rules of thumb by a wide margin.
   a. True.
   b. False.

9. *Identify* two major routes leading from forecast to portfolio construction.

10. Briefly *explain* the relationship between real returns on high-grade bonds and inflation. Then *explain* the relationship between real returns on stocks and inflation.

11. *Discuss* why bond volatility is easier to predict than stock volatility.

12. From the perspective of bond managers, *identify* three important outputs of a macroeconomic forecast.

13. According to Dialynas, the most potent way to add value to a bond portfolio is through:
    a. Issue selection.
    b. Sector selection.
    c. Using a duration strategy.
    d. State-of-the-art quantitative analysis.

14. Which of the following are attributes of a bond portfolio's risk?
    i.   duration
    ii. convexity
    iii. sector distribution
    iv. yield curve distribution
    v.   credit quality
    a. i and ii only.
    b. i, iii, and iv only.
    c. ii, iii, and v only.
    d. i, ii, iii, iv, and v.

15. *List* at least two reasons prepayment forecasts are important in fixed-income security selection.

16. Briefly *explain* how economic growth results in a "transfer effect" and an "income effect" that influences mortgage prepayments.

17. Which of the following are important economic time series for mortgage-backed security valuation?
    i.   interest rates
    ii. housing starts
    iii. consumer confidence
    iv. gross domestic product
    v.   personal income
    a. i and v only.
    b. ii, iii, and iv only.
    c. i, ii, iii, and v only.
    d. i, ii, iii, iv, and v.

18. *List* the four major factors that move the stock market, and *identify* which factor is most important.

19. According to Garzarelli, the market rarely goes above its fair value because it is highly efficient.
    a. True.
    b. False.

20. *List* four strategic asset allocation techniques.

21. *Identify* the three stages of a standardized valuation model.

22. According to Diermeier, all the following are major challenges in global portfolio construction except:
    a. Real growth analysis.
    b. Currency allocation.
    c. Risky asset allocation.
    d. Decision hierarchy (country versus security).

23. According to Clough, a worldwide credit contraction is under way.
    a. True.
    b. False.

24. Clough expects both financial market returns and cash returns will be higher in the 1990s than in the 1980s.
    a. True.
    b. False.

25. Clough contends that the worldwide cost of capital is falling. Briefly *explain* what impact a lower cost of capital might have on the relationship between labor and capital for corporations.

Self-Evaluation Answers

1. Economics cannot be subject to complete quantification as a science because of the human element. The art-form aspect reflects the blending of statistical facts with judgments about human behavior on the basis of insights derived from experience and intuition. See Bostian.

2. Three major risks in economic forecasting are:
   - Human weaknesses (linear perception, group think, and the messenger syndrome).
   - Faulty or inaccurate economic data.
   - Faulty economic theories.

   See Bostian.

3. True. Rate of change is a good method for expressing a discipline for forecasting the economic cycle. See Bostian.

4. The Bostian Macro-Economic Index (MEI) differs from the Leading Economic Indicators (LEI) as follows:
   - The MEI has 26 independent variables versus 11 for the LEI.
   - LEI does not include profits and interest rates.
   - The MEI uses a rate of change basis.

   See Bostian.

5. True. Make the domestic forecast first and then make changes based on international considerations. See Bostian.

6. True. See McNees.

7. Forecasting accuracy has improved over time because of:
   - More and better data.
   - Improved forecasting techniques.
   - Changes in the structure of the economy.
   - More competition among forecasters.

   See McNees.

8. False. See McNees.

9. Two routes leading from forecast to portfolio construction are:
   - Developing a capital market line to show the risk–return trade-off among various assets.
   - Estimating the expected equity risk premium or the excess equity returns over bond returns.

   If the spread is wider than normal, buy stocks and sell bonds. See Bernstein.

10. Real returns on high-grade bonds are a function of inflation. These returns are good when inflation is low or deflation exists, but they are poor when the price level is rising rapidly.

    There is no consistent relationship between stocks and inflation or deflation. The performance of stocks has been good and bad under both scenarios. See Bernstein.

11. There is a close relationship between bond volatility and inflation. Stock volatility is a function of the whole economic system. See Bernstein.

12. Important outputs of a macroeconomic forecast are:
    - Interest rate forecast.
    - Set of volatility assessments.
    - Forecast of consumer spending and personal finance behavior.
    - Forecast of capital structure trends.
    - Forecast for the real and financial economics of other important countries.

    See Dialynas.

13. The most potent way to add value to a bond portfolio is through using a duration strategy. See Dialynas.

14. d. All of the factors are attributes of a bond portfolio's risk. See Dialynas.

15. Prepayment forecasts are important because they:
    - Determine cash flow patterns for the securities, which will affect the yield, the holding period return, and the effective duration of the securities.
    - Are required for option-adjusted spread analysis.
    - Can overpower interest rate predictions.

    See Kopprasch.

16. The transfer effect occurs as workers move to areas having economic growth. The income effect leads homeowners to increase their housing expenditures by trading up to more expensive housing. Both effects generate prepayments. See Kopprasch.

17. c. Interest rates, housing starts, consumer confidence, and personal income are important. See Kopprasch.

18. The four major factors that move the stock market are:
    - ▓ The economy (earnings, industrial production, real gross domestic product on a change basis).
    - ▓ Federal Reserve policy (discount rate).
    - ▓ Valuation.
    - ▓ Sentiment.

    Garzarelli notes that each factor makes up about 25 percent of the market movement. Overall, no single factor is most important. See Garzarelli.

19. False. See Garzarelli.

20. Four strategic asset allocation techniques are:
    - ▓ Comparative valuation.
    - ▓ Business cycle anticipation (leading indicators).
    - ▓ Liquidity/flow of funds.
    - ▓ Technical analysis.

    See Diermeier.

21. The three stages of a standardized valuation model are:
    - ▓ Discounted value in growth-to-normal stage.
    - ▓ Discounted value in normal growth stage.
    - ▓ Discounted value in mature stage.

    See Diermeier.

22. a. Real growth analysis is not a major challenge in global portfolio construction. See Diermeier.

23. True. See Clough.

24. False. See Clough.

25. Because the cost of labor is high, corporations have an incentive to reduce the labor component of costs. Thus, they would substitute capital for labor in a low cost of capital world. See Clough.

Order Form ₀₁₇

Additional copies of *Improving the Investment Decision Process—Better Use of Economic Inputs in Securities Analysis and Portfolio Management* (and other AIMR publications listed on page 76) are available for purchase. The price is **$20 each in U.S. dollars**. Simply complete this form and return it via mail or fax to:

AIMR
Publications Sales Department
P.O. Box 7947
Charlottesville, Va. 22906
U.S.A.
Telephone: 804/980-3647
Fax: 804/977-0350

Name _____

Company _____

Address _____

_____ Suite/Floor _____

City _____

State _____ ZIP _____ Country _____

Daytime Telephone _____

Title of Publication	Price	Qty.	Total
_____	____	____	____
_____	____	____	____

Shipping/Handling
- ❑ All U.S. orders: Included in price of book
- ❑ Air mail, Canada and Mexico: $5 per book
- ❑ Surface mail, Canada and Mexico: $3 per book
- ❑ Air mail, all other countries: $8 per book
- ❑ Surface mail, all other countries: $6 per book

Discounts
- ❑ Students, professors, university libraries: 25%
- ❑ CFA candidates (ID #_____): 25%
- ❑ Retired members (ID #_____): 25%
- ❑ Volume orders (50+ books of same title): 40%

Discount $-_____

4.5% sales tax
(Virginia residents) $_____

8.25% sales tax
(New York residents) $_____

7% GST
(Canada residents,
#124134602) $_____

Shipping/handling $_____

Total cost of order $_____

❑ Check or money order enclosed payable to **AIMR**   ❑ Invoice me
Charge to: ❑ VISA   ❑ MASTERCARD   ❑ AMERICAN EXPRESS

Card Number:_____ ❑ Corporate ❑ Personal

Signature:_____ Expiration date: _____

Selected AIMR Publications*

Ethics, Fairness, Efficiency, and Financial Markets, 1992 . . . . $20
  Hersh Shefrin and Meir Statman

Investing Worldwide III, 1992 . . . . $20

**The Financial Services Industry—Banks, Thrifts, Insurance
  Companies, and Securities Firms**, 1992 . . . . $20
  Alfred C. Morley, CFA, *Editor*

Managing Asset/Liability Portfolios, 1992 . . . . $20
  Eliot P. Williams, CFA, *Editor*

Investing for the Long Term, 1992 . . . . $20

A New Method for Valuing Treasury Bond Futures Options, 1992 . . . . $20
  Ehud I. Ronn and Robert R. Bliss, Jr.

Ethics in the Investment Profession: A Survey, 1992 . . . . $20
  E. Theodore Veit, CFA, and Michael R. Murphy, CFA

The Transportation Industry—Airlines, Trucking, and Railroads, 1992 . . . . $20
  David G. Smith, *Editor*

Earnings Forecasts and Share Price Reversals, 1992 . . . . $20
  Werner F.M. De Bondt

The CFA Study Guide, 1993 (Level I, Level II, or Level III) . . . . $20 each

**Corporate Bond Rating Drift: An Examination of Credit
  Quality Rating Changes Over Time**, 1991 . . . . $20
  Edward I. Altman and Duen Li Kao

Investing Worldwide II (1991), **Investing Worldwide** (1990) . . . . $20 each

Managing the Investment Firm, 1991 . . . . $20
  James R. Vertin, CFA, *Editor*

**The Founders of Modern Finance: Their Prize-winning
  Concepts and 1990 Nobel Lectures**, 1991 . . . . $20

**The Poison Pill Anti-takeover Defense: The Price of Strategic
  Deterrence**, 1991 . . . . $20
  Robert F. Bruner

**Performance Reporting for Investment Managers: Applying the
  AIMR Performance Presentation Standards**, 1991 . . . . $20

Initiating and Managing a Global Investment Program, 1991 . . . . $20
  William G. Droms, CFA, *Editor*

*A full catalog of publications is available from AIMR, P.O. Box 7947, Charlottesville, Va. 22906; 804/980-3647; fax 804/977-0350.